The Logic
of Liberty

Michael Polanyi

The Logic of Liberty

REFLECTIONS AND REJOINDERS

Michael Polanyi

Foreword by Stuart D. Warner

LIBERTY FUND

Licensed by the University of Chicago Press, Chicago, Illinois
© Published under the International Copyright Union.
All rights reserved. Published 1951.

Frontispiece: Michael Polanyi, c. 1915. Courtesy of the Special
Collections Department of the University of Chicago Library.

Foreword © 1998 by Liberty Fund, Inc. All rights reserved.
Printed in the United States of America

98 17 18 19 20 C 5 4 3 2 1
17 18 19 20 21 P 6 5 4 3 2

LIBRARY OF CONGRESS CATALOGING-IN-PUBLICATION DATA
Polanyi, Michael, 1891–
The logic of liberty : reflections and rejoinders / Michael Polanyi :
foreword by Stuart Warner.
p. cm.
Originally published: London : Routledge and K. Paul, 1951 in series:
International library of sociology and social reconstruction (Routledge
& Kegan Paul).
Includes bibliographical references and index.
ISBN 0-86597-182-X (alk. paper).—ISBN 0-86597-183-8
(pbk. : alk. paper)
1. Liberty.   2. Research.   I. Title.
HM271.P6   1998
303.48′3—dc21   98-5301

LIBERTY FUND, INC.
11301 North Meridian Street
Carmel, Indiana 46032

Contents

Foreword

Michael Polanyi was born in Budapest in 1891, and he died in 1976. His university studies initially centered on medicine, but he soon turned his attention to chemistry. By the early 1930s he had published more than one hundred seventy-five technical papers in the physical sciences and had held research positions in Germany at the Kaiser Wilhelm Institute for Fibre Chemistry and at the Institute for Physical Chemistry. In 1933 he left Germany to become chair of physical chemistry at Manchester University. At a relatively young age Polanyi had been interested in the political life of Europe, and this interest intensified during the 1930s, as European civilization trembled before its future, and during the 1940s, as Europeans looked wistfully upon their past.

In 1938 Louis Rougier, inspired by Walter Lippmann's *An Inquiry into the Principles of a Good Society,* organized a meeting in Paris with the idea of forming an intellectual society that would strive to restore the ideals of classical liberalism. Polanyi was one of the twenty-six participants in that meeting; others included Raymond Aron, F. A. Hayek, and Ludwig von Mises. The society became moribund during the Second World War, but Hayek reclaimed the idea, and in 1947 he began the Mont Pelerin Society. Polanyi was one of the Mont Pelerin Society's sixty-four founding members, as were Bertrand de Jouvenel, Karl Popper, Hans Barth,

Carlo Antoni, Milton Friedman, George Stigler, Frank Knight, and C. V. Wedgwood.

Though Polanyi continued writing scientific articles until 1949, their numbers began to diminish by the mid-1930s as he turned his intellectual energies to reflections about things human. A crucial experience in his intellectual pilgrimage occurred in 1935 when he visited Russia. What struck Polanyi most profoundly during his trip was Nikolai Bukharin's insistence that there was no real meaning to the distinction between pure and applied science—that science had value only when it furthered practical and material ends. Indeed, Bukharin argued that the very fabric of science *must* be sewn out of things practical and material, because it was the practical in life that was always responsible for scientific reflection. Believing that this instrumentalist conception represented a dangerous misunderstanding of science, and that it was gaining acceptance even in England where he lived, Polanyi wrote a series of articles in opposition to it and in support of the idea of the propriety of pure theoretical science.

Polanyi's reflections on the nature of science were first prompted and marked by the contingent circumstances of his own time; however, these reflections quickly assumed a distinctively philosophical cast, and they achieved their most acute understanding in *Personal Knowledge* (1958). The philosophical movement of Polanyi's thought endeavored to understand science as a model for an appreciably broader range of human activities—indeed, as a model for understanding some fundamental elements of the human situation. Polanyi's turn to philosophy eventually led to his appointment in 1948 as chair of social studies at Manchester.

The Logic of Liberty, first published in 1951, consists of a series of articles, all but one of which were written after the Second World War. Polanyi states in the preface that the book represents his "consistently renewed efforts to clarify the position of liberty in response to a number of questions raised by our troubled period of history." This statement, coupled with the fact that several of the articles are rejoinders to the defenders of an instrumentalist conception of science, might tempt us to think the book dated or parochial. This is a temptation to be resisted, for that conception would be a wholly inadequate understanding of the character and temper of Polanyi's book. As the very title of the work indicates, Polanyi's overriding concern was how best to understand the fundamental structure of liberty. This is a perennial concern. He explores the subject both directly—especially in the second half of the book—and indirectly. This indirect line of inquiry reflects his desire to understand those contemporary movements—both theoretical and practical— that were inimical to liberty. In this regard, Polanyi believed that if he could grasp at least part of the reason why liberty was being eclipsed, he would at the same time indirectly comprehend more about the logic of liberty itself.

The Logic of Liberty explores the structure of *public* liberty. Polanyi's understanding of public liberty turns on his conception of the forms of social order. There is a general tendency to think that all social order has been intentionally designed or achieved by some one person or group. Against this tendency, Polanyi holds that the social orders most important to human well-being are *spontaneous* orders, that is, orders that result from the interplay of individuals mutually adjusting their actions to the actions of others. Spontaneous orders are the result of human action but not of human design. Polanyi recognizes the economic market as a leading exemplar of such an order, and he points to Adam Smith as someone who insightfully articulated the logic of that order.

However, what fascinates Polanyi more, and what he finds ultimately more revealing about liberty, are *intellectual* spontaneous orders, especially science.

Science is a spontaneous order, both in terms of the activity of science itself and the results of scientific inquiry. Through consultation, competition, and persuasion, scientists, moved by their own initiative, adjust their lines of investigation and judgment to the lines of investigation and judgment of other scientists. Polanyi believes, however, that for there to be a scientific order something more is needed —a channeling "device" through which the diverse actions of scientists are coordinated. This "device" is the goal, or end, of science, and Polanyi identifies this end as the pursuit of truth. For Polanyi, it is in the belief in the transcendent reality of truth that science has its extraordinary character as an intellectual *system*.

Science is not only Polanyi's most important model of an intellectual spontaneous order, but it is also his most important model of a *public* liberty. The idea of public liberty is the most important concept in *The Logic of Liberty*—and it is also the most difficult to grasp. The difficulty lies in the fact that liberty today is most often thought of as either the rights of individuals to pursue private courses of action, or political liberties such as voting. The liberty Polanyi elucidates is something very different.

By "public liberty" Polanyi means a *liberty* the exercise of which contributes to the formation or maintenance of a spontaneous order. In the case of science, the liberty Polanyi speaks of refers to the activity of scientists acting on the basis of their own initiative in their attempts to understand the truth. Polanyi cites the common law as another example of an intellectual spontaneous order and, thus, as another example of a public liberty. Liberty here refers to the activity of judges adjusting their decisions to the decisions of other judges in order to arrive at a determination of justice.

What principally marks these liberties as *public* liberties is that the scientist and judge are acting as members of *public* institutions, namely, science and law. Indeed, it is because of the public benefits resulting from their actions that we accord the scientist and the judge the liberty to act on the basis of their own initiatives—subject, of course, to limitations inherent in the activities of science and judging that make them possible: public liberty is not public license. The liberty of the scientist and judge implicates them in a public trust—through partaking in a public institution, they have a fiduciary responsibility to the public. On this analysis of liberty, therefore, liberty and responsibility are inextricably intertwined.

Polanyi states in his preface that he champions a free society and not an "open" one. The distinction he draws is important because, to Polanyi, a free society, unlike an "open" one, is "dedicated to a distinctive set of beliefs," namely, belief in the transcendent realities of truth, justice, charity, and toleration. It is belief in such realities, belief that constitutes a moral commitment incapable of proof, that characterizes a free society, and it is belief in such realities that makes public liberties both possible and justifiable. What Polanyi emphasizes is that a free society is characterized less by its private liberties and more by its public ones and its shared beliefs in a public realm.

A detailed consideration of what underlies a variety of criticisms of public liberty in Polanyi's time figures prominently in his elucidation of his idea of public liberty. Science is Polanyi's principal model of public liberty; science is also his principal model of public liberty under attack. The criticism of theoretical science levied by totalitarianism is anchored, Polanyi believes, in a materialistic view of human nature that rejects those realities—truth, justice, charity, and toleration—on which public liberty rests. The rejection of those realities leads to a conception of science as instrumental, and this conception requires that science be used in the service of material ends. In the hands of those who subscribe to the "virtues" of planned science, the activities of scientists should be directly prescribed by the State. Science as a public liberty is thus subverted. Indeed, under totalitarianism all public liberties are subverted: the State controls all "public" avenues of life. In this way, the power of the State becomes the only source of order and the adjudicator of all conflicts and disagreements, including intellectual ones, as evidenced by the Lysenko affair.

Obviously, totalitarianism relentlessly undermines liberty. Many who consider this fact focus on private liberty—individuals cannot pursue their own desires quite so readily, to say nothing of being subjected to sheer brutality. Although Polanyi surely recognizes this, he emphasizes instead the manner in which public liberty is eclipsed in totalitarian regimes. Motivating him here is his understanding that public liberty forms the inescapable foundation of a free society, a foundation that provides the conditions under which private liberty can achieve some degree of social efficacy. However, it is not, Polanyi thinks, only totalitarian movements that threaten public liberty. All movements of thought and practice that attempt to render spontaneous orders nugatory—that are captured by the idea that all social order either is or should be planned—also threaten public liberty and, thus, threaten the fabric of a free society.

That a free society—one in which public liberty reigns—and a good society—one animated by a belief in transcendent realities—are of a piece occupies a central place in *The*

Logic of Liberty. Given this, and the argument of the preceding paragraph, one might expect Polanyi to declare that moral considerations are absent in totalitarian regimes. What Polanyi finds peculiar about totalitarianism is that despite its rejection of transcendent reality, it exhibits a high degree of moral passion. This moral passion, however, is not a mark of honor—instead, it is a mark of dishonor. Polanyi argues that the moral passions that in fact can animate totalitarianism—and also some of the less-virulent strains of human folly—have become unhinged from any reality that could restrain them. Here we have moral passion without any moral judgment. Polanyi maintains that a "moral inversion" has occurred: moral passion now invokes any means, however grotesque and *immoral,* to satisfy its longings. Under this guise, moral passion serves rather than spurns the cause of fanaticism. That is a cause which continues in our own times to pose a threat to the liberty that is the subject of Polanyi's book.

Stuart D. Warner

Preface

It is unfortunate that not until we have unsystematically collected observations for a long time to serve as building materials, following the guidance of an idea which lies concealed in our minds, and indeed only after we have spent much time in the technical disposition of these materials, do we first become capable of viewing the idea in a clearer light and of outlining it architectonically as one whole according to the intentions of reason.

KANT, *Critique of Pure Reason*

These pieces were written in the course of the last eight years. They represent my consistently renewed efforts to clarify the position of liberty in response to a number of questions raised by our troubled period of history. One aspect of liberty after another was reconsidered, as in the course of time each in turn revealed its vulnerability. This dialectic has covered a fair range of relevant issues and has, I believe, evoked some valid answers, proved in battle. I have thought of melting down the material and casting it into a mould of a comprehensive system, but this seemed premature. It cannot be attempted without establishing first a better foundation than we possess to-day for the holding of our beliefs.

But I hope that my collection may supply some elements of a future coherent doctrine, since it expresses throughout a consistent line of thought. I take more seriously here than was done in the past the fiduciary presuppositions of science; that is the fact that our discovery and acceptance of scientific knowledge is a commitment to certain beliefs which we hold, but which others may refuse to share. Freedom in science appears then as the Natural Law of a community committed to certain beliefs and the same is seen to apply by analogy to other kinds of intellectual liberty. On these lines, freedom of thought is justified in general to the extent to which we believe in the power of thought and recognize our obligation to cultivate the things of the mind. Once committed to such beliefs and obligations we must uphold freedom, but in doing so freedom is not our primary consideration.

Economic liberty I regard as a social technique suitable, and indeed indispensable, for the administration of a particular productive technique. While we are deeply committed to this technology to-day, other alternatives may one day present themselves with strong claims in their favour.

Freedom of the individual to do as he pleases, so long as he respects the other fellow's right to do likewise, plays only a minor part in this theory of freedom. Private individualism is no important pillar of public liberty. A free society is not an Open Society, but one fully dedicated to a distinctive set of beliefs.

There is a link between my insistence on acknowledging the fiduciary foundations of science and thought in general, and my rejection of the individualistic formula of liberty. This formula could be upheld only in the innocence of eighteenth-century rationalism, with its ingenuous self-evidences and unshakable scientific truths. Modern liberty, which has to stand up to a total critique of its fiduciary foundations, will have to be conceived in more positive terms. Its claims must be closely circumscribed and at the same time sharpened for a defence against new opponents, incomparably more formidable than those against which liberty achieved its first victories in the gentler centuries of modern Europe.

I believe that these comprehensive questions cannot be handled with detachment, but that their treatment requires the full participation of the writer in the issues which form his subject. I have included therefore some addresses delivered on controversial occasions.

ACKNOWLEDGMENTS

The author wishes to thank the editors of the following publications for permission to make use in this book of articles, or portions of articles, which first appeared in their pages:

Advancement of Science, Archiv der Staatswissenschaften, The Bulletin of the Atomic Scientists, Economica, Humanitas, The Lancet, The Listener, Measure, Memoirs and Proceedings of the Manchester Literary and Philosophical Society, The Nineteenth Century, The Political Quarterly, The Scientific Monthly.

M. P.

PART I

The Example of Science

1

Social Message of Pure Science[1] (1945)

Applied science has a clear purpose: it serves our welfare and security. But what about pure science? What justification is there in scientific studies which have no visible practical use? Until fairly recently it used to be commonly assumed that such studies served their own purpose, the discovery of knowledge for the love of truth. Do we still accept that view? Do we still believe that it is proper for a scientist to spend public funds for the pursuit

1. In August 1938 the British Association for the Advancement of Science founded a new Division for the Social and International Relations of Science, which was largely motivated from the start by the desire to give deliberate social guidance to the progress of science. This movement gathered considerable momentum throughout the following years, so that when the Division met in December 1945 for a discussion on the Planning of Science, I expected the meeting to be overwhelmingly in favour of planning. My opening address, *The Social Message of Pure Science,* was written with this prospect in mind, but actually the occasion proved a turning point. Speakers and audience showed themselves consistently in favour of the traditional position of pure science, pursued freely for its own sake. Since then the movement for the planning of science has rapidly declined to insignificance in Britain.

3

of studies such as, say, the proof of Fermat's theorem—or the counting of the number of electrons in the universe: studies which, though perhaps not lacking in some remote possibility of practical usefulness, are at any rate as unlikely to yield a material dividend as any human activity within the realms of sanity? No, we do not generally accept the view today, as we did until the nineteen-thirties, that it is proper for science to pursue knowledge for its own sake, regardless of any advantage to the welfare of society. Nor is the change due to altered circumstances, but it represents a fundamental turn of popular opinion, induced by a definite philosophical movement of recent times.

The philosophical movement which has thus called in question the traditional standing of science, has launched its attack from two different sides. One line of attack is directed against the claim of science to speak in its own right. This is the line of modern materialistic analysis, which denies that the human intellect can operate independently on its own grounds and holds that the purpose of thought is, at bottom, always practical. Science in this view is merely an ideology, the contents of which are determined by social needs. The development of science is then explained by the successive rise of new practical interests. Newton, for example, is represented as discovering gravitation in response to rising navigational interests and Maxwell as discovering the electromagnetic field stimulated by the need for transatlantic communications. Such a philosophy denies that pure science has a purpose in itself and wipes out the distinction between pure and applied science. Pure science is then valued mainly for not being altogether pure—for the fact that it may turn out to be useful in the end.

The other line of attack is based on moral grounds. It insists that scientists should turn their eyes to the misery which fills the world and think of the relief they could bring to it. It asks whether, on looking round, they can find it in their hearts to use their gifts for the mere elucidation of some abstruse problem—the counting of the electrons in the universe, or the solution of Fermat's theorem. Could they possibly prove so selfish . . . ? Scientists are morally reproached for pursuing science for the mere love of knowledge.

Thus we can see the position of pure science to-day under the crossfire of two attacks based on rather disparate grounds; forming a somewhat paradoxical combination— but one that is actually typical of the modern mind. A new destructive scepticism is linked here to a new passionate social conscience; an utter disbelief in the spirit of man is coupled with extravagant moral demands. We see at work here the form of action which has already dealt so many shattering blows to the modern world: the chisel of scepticism driven by the hammer of social passion.

This recalls the wider implications of our problem, revealed by the spectacle of Europe. The destruction of our civilization over large stretches of the Continent was not due to some accidental outbursts of Fascist beastliness. The events which, starting from the Russian Revolution, have ravaged the Continent represent on the contrary a single coherent process: one vast general upheaval. Great waves of humanitarian and patriotic sentiments were its prime impulses, and it was these sentiments which actuated the destruction of Europe. Savagery is always there lurking among us; but it can break loose on a grand scale only when rebellious moral passions first break up the controls of civilization. There are always some potential Hitlers and Mussolinis about, but they can gain power only if they succeed in perverting moral forces to their own ends.

We must ask, therefore, why moral forces could be thus perverted?; why the great social passions of our time were turned into violent and destructive channels? The answer can only be that there was no other channel available to them. A radical scepticism had destroyed popular belief in the reality of justice and reason. It had stamped these ideas as mere superstructures; as out-of-date ideologies of a bourgeois age; as mere screens for selfish interests hiding behind them; and indeed, as sources of confusion and weakness to anyone who would trust in them.

There was no sufficiently strong belief in justice and reason left in which to embody social passions. A generation grew up full of moral fire and yet despising reason and justice. Believing instead in what?—in the forces which were left for them to believe in—in Power, Economic Interest, Subconscious Desire. These they accepted therefore as the ultimate reality to which they could entrust themselves. Here they found a modern, acid-proof embodiment for their moral aspirations. Compassion was turned into merciless hatred and the desire for brotherhood into deadly class-war. Patriotism was turned into Fascist beastliness; the more evil, the more patriotic were the people who had gone Fascist.

Mr. Attlee recently described the most urgent need in Europe at the present time: "We need," he said, "a conception of justice not as a will of a section, but as something absolute" and a leadership "which will lift people up from a mere longing for material benefits to a sense of the highest mission of mankind." Mr. Bevin has spoken in a similar fashion when, facing the starving masses of Europe, he talked of a "spiritual hunger which is even more devastating than physical hunger."

But unfortunately, the doctrine which was so effectively hammered into our heads by the leading philosophical movement during the past generation taught precisely this: that justice is nothing but the will of one section; and that there can be nothing higher than the longing for material benefits—so that to talk about higher missions is just foolishness or deceit. The most urgent need of the day is to oppose this philosophy at every point. To us scientists it falls to attack it in connection with science. The most vital service we owe to the world to-day is to restore our own scientific ideals which have fallen into discredit under the influence of the modern philosophical movement. We must reassert that the essence of science is the love of knowledge and that the utility of knowledge does not concern us primarily. We should demand once more for science that public respect and support which is due to it as a pursuit of knowledge and of knowledge alone. For we scientists are pledged to values more precious than material welfare and to a service more urgent than that of material welfare.

How sharply the spirit of pure scholarship is opposed to the claims of totalitarianism has been sufficiently proven on many cruel occasions during contemporary history. Universities which upheld the purity of their standards under totalitarianism invariably had to stand up to harsh pressure and often suffered heavy penalties. The whole world recognizes to-day its debt to universities in Poland and Norway, in Holland, Belgium and France, where such pressure was withstood and such penalties endured. These places are witnesses to-day to the convictions underlying our European civilization and hold out the hope of a genuine European recovery. And where, on the contrary, universities have allowed themselves to be cajoled or terrorized into compromising their standards, we feel that the very roots of our civilization have been marred. In such places our hopes for the future burn low.

The world needs science to-day above all as an example of the good life. Spread out over the planet scientists form even to-day, though submerged by disaster, the body of a great and good society. Even at present scientists of Moscow and Cambridge, of Bangalore and San Francisco, respect the same standards in science; and in the depths of shattered Germany and Japan a scientist is still one of ourselves, upholding the same code of scientific work. Isolated though we are to-day from each other, we still bear the mark of a common intellectual heritage and claim succession to the same great forerunners.

Such is my conception of the relation of science to the community in our days. In the great struggle for our civilization science occupies a section in the front line. In the movement which is undermining the position of pure science I see one detachment of the forces assailing our whole civilization. I have said that these forces embody some of the most enterprising and generous sentiments of our days—but that makes them only the more dangerous in my eyes. We shall have to fight in this battle some of the best motives of human progress. But we cannot afford to be deflected by them. The easy wisdom of the modern sceptic, destroying the spiritual guidance of man and setting free so much untutored enthusiasm, has cost us too dearly already. Whatever scorn be poured upon us by those who find our faith in pure science old-fashioned, and whatever condemnation by others who think us selfish, we must persist in vindicating the ideals of science.

2

Scientific Convictions[1]

I

There are many jokes about the futility of philosophizing, and it is true that science is a much more business-like occupation in which every achievement, however modest, may give you sound satisfaction. For there your work stands, public, compelling and permanent; it testifies that for one moment you were allowed to make intellectual history. You have disclosed something that had never been known before and that—you may hope—will henceforth continue to be known as long as the memory of our civilization endures.

Some philosophers of the last century were so much impressed by this kind of positive achievement, that they decided to liquidate philosophy altogether and divide up its subject-matter among different sciences. A number of new sciences which took man or human affairs as their subject, were formed at that time and appeared to serve this purpose. Psychology and Sociology were acclaimed as the principal legatees in this sharing out of the substance of philosophy.

---

1. Expanded from *The Nineteenth Century,* 1949.

This philosophy-to-end-all-philosophy may be designated, if somewhat loosely, as Positivism. It continued in the nineteenth and twentieth centuries the rebellion against the authority of the Christian Churches, first started in the days of Montaigne, Bacon and Descartes; but it set out not only to liberate reason from enslavement by authority, but also to dispose of all traditionally guiding ideas, so far as they were not demonstrable by science. Thus, in the positivist sense truth became identified with scientific truth and the latter tended to be defined—by a positivist critique of science—as a mere ordering of experience.

Justice, morality, custom and law now appear as mere sets of conventions, charged with emotional approval, which are the proper study of sociology. Conscience is identified with the fear of breaking socially approved conventions and its investigation is assigned to psychology. Aesthetic values are related to an equilibrium of opposed impulses in the nervous system of the beholder.[2] In the positivist theory, man is a system responding regularly to a certain range of stimuli. The prisoner tortured by his gaolers in order to extract from him the names of his confederates, and similarly, the gaolers torturing him for this purpose, are both merely registering adequate responses to their situations.

Under the guidance of such concepts we are expected to become truly detached and objective in our approach to the whole world, including our own selves and all the affairs of men. Scientific man shall master both his inner conflicts and those of his social environment and, set free from metaphysical delusions, henceforth refuse to submit to any obligations that cannot be demonstrated to lie in his proper interest.

2. Only the last item on this list requires supporting evidence, for which see I. A. Richards, *The Principles of Literary Criticism* (1924), pp. 245, 251 (1930 ed.).

Such a programme implies, of course, that science itself is "positive," in the sense that it involves no affirmation of personal beliefs. Since this is in fact untrue—as it is my purpose to show here—it is not surprising that the positivist movement, having first exalted science to the seat of universal arbitrament, now threatens to overthrow and destroy it. The tension between Marxism and science, which has made its appearance in Soviet Russia and has become steadily more intense during the past fifteen years, is a manifestation of this threat, and a logical consequence of the conflict between the aspirations of positivism and the true nature of science.

II

We shall get our own attitude to science into better perspective if we digress for a moment on some kinds of knowledge forming no part of science and held to be erroneous by most of us. Take sorcery and astrology. I shall assume that these are both held to be false by the reader; but obviously the same does not hold for everybody even to-day. Sorcery, for example, is being practised among primitive people throughout the planet. In order to bewitch somebody, the sorcerer gets hold of an appurtenance of his victim, such as a lock of hair, a bone he had spit out, or any excretion of his, and burns this object, pronouncing a curse on its owner. This is believed to be effective and it is common among primitive communities to ascribe the incidence of death invariably to the effects of sorcery.

Now if we ask, "What is sorcery?" clearly we cannot say that "it is the destruction of human beings by burning a lock of their hair, etc.," for we do not believe that man can be killed by such means. We have to say, "There is a belief in sorcery, which we do not share and which affirms the possibility of killing a man by burning a lock of his hair." And similarly, we cannot define astrology as a method for predicting the course of men's lives by casting their horoscopes, but could only describe it as a belief—which we do not share—in the possibility of foretelling the future from the stars.

Naturally, a sorcerer or an astrologer would speak differently. The first may state that sorcery is the way of killing a man by burning a lock of his hair, or the like; the second will describe astrology as the art of predicting the future from horoscopes. However, if pressed by our scepticism, they would be prepared no doubt to recast their accounts of sorcery or astrology into a statement similar in form to our own definition, but replacing the words, "a belief which we do not share," by the expression, "a belief which we share." And on these grounds we could both agree to differ.

All this has its obvious application to science. Any account of science which does not explicitly describe it as something we believe in, is essentially incomplete and a false pretension. It amounts to a claim that science is essentially different from and superior to all human beliefs which are not scientific statements, and this is untrue.

To show the falsity of this pretension, it should suffice to recall that originality is the mainspring of scientific discovery. Originality in science is the gift of a lonely belief in a line of experiments or of speculations, which at the time no one else considered to be profitable. Scientists spend all their time betting their lives, bit by bit, on one personal belief after the other. The moment discovery is claimed, the lonely belief now made public and the evidence produced in its favour, evoke a response among scientists which is another belief, a public belief, that can range over all grades of acceptance or rejection. Whether any particular discovery is recognized and developed further, or discouraged and perhaps even smothered at birth, will depend on the kind of belief or disbelief which it evokes among scientific opinion.

Take for example the fanciful suggestion described a little later (p. 20) of connecting the period of gestation of animals with the multiples of the number π. Its unhesitant rejection by science represents a comparatively recent point of view in science. To a scientist like Kepler there would have been nothing repugnant in the relationship suggested here. He himself derived the existence of the then known seven planets and the relative size of their orbits from the existence of seven perfect solids and the relative sizes of their inscribed and enveloping spheres, the edges of the solids being of constant length. The science of his generation was still largely pursuing the Pythagorean supposition of a world governed by number rules and geometrical relationships. The terms in which science interpreted nature at that time are no longer believed in to-day.

It would take me too long to trace here in detail the successive stages through which the premises of science have passed from Kepler's day to our own. The main period from Galileo to Young, Fresnel and Faraday was dominated by the idea of a mechanical universe consisting of matter in motion. This was modified by the field theories of Faraday and Maxwell, but not radically changed as long as the postulate of a material ether was upheld. Until the end of the nineteenth century, scientists believed implicitly in the mechanical explanation of all phenomena. In the last fifty years these premises of science were abandoned, but not without causing considerable delay in the progress of discoveries which were inaccessible from such premises. A good deal of evidence for the existence of the electron had been available for a long time before it overcame the resistance offered by the assumption that all properties of matter had to be explained by mass in motion.

An entirely new supposition, based on Mach's philosophy, was imported into science by Einstein in his discovery of relativity. Mach had set out to eliminate all tautologies from scientific statements; Einstein assumed that by modifying our conceptions of space and time on the lines of such a programme, it should be possible to draw up a system which would eliminate some existing anomalies and possibly lead to new verifiable conclusions. This is the epistemological method which is profoundly ingrained to-day in our conception of the universe.

The firmness of our belief in the new epistemologically sifted conception of space and time may be illustrated by the following event. In 1925 the American physicist D. C. Milner repeated, for the first time after a generation, Michelson's experiment on which the theory of relativity was originally based. Equipped with the most modern instruments, he thought he had a right to check up on these rather hoary observations of a great master. His results contradicted those of Michelson and he announced this to a representative gathering of physicists. But not one of them thought for a moment of abandoning relativity. Instead—as Sir Charles Darwin once described it—they sent Milner home to get his results right.

The day-to-day function exercised by scientific beliefs in regulating the response made by scientists to current publications, may be further illustrated by a pair of instances which provide an interesting comparison. In 1947 two papers came out almost simultaneously by two authoritative physicists in Britain, the reception of which by scientific opinion formed a striking contrast. One paper was published in the *Proceedings of the Royal Society* in June 1947, by Lord Rayleigh, a distinguished Fellow of the Society. It described some simple experiments which proved in the author's opinion that a hydrogen atom impinging on a metal wire could transmit to it energies ranging up to a hundred electron-volts. Such an observation, if correct, would be of immense importance. Far more revolutionary, for example, than the discovery of atomic fission by Otto Hahn in 1939. Yet when this paper appeared and I asked various physicists' opinions about it, they only shrugged their shoulders. They could not find fault with the experiment, yet not one believed in its results, nor thought it even worth while to repeat it. They just ignored it. Since Lord Rayleigh has since died, the matter seems to have been already forgotten.

About simultaneously with Lord Rayleigh's paper (May 1947), Professor P. M. S. Blackett published the fact that a simple relationship between angular momentum and stellar magnetism was applicable to the Earth, the Sun and a third star, the data for which lie over a wide range of values. This communication, though meagre as compared with Rayleigh's and not of obvious significance, was received as an important discovery. Its reception was indeed quite exceptional. The original address was published by *Nature* in full length immediately after its delivery to the Royal Society and the daily press brought long extracts of it with facsimiles of Blackett's proposed formula in his own handwriting. No greater attention could be concentrated on a new contribution to science.

I feel sure that thirty years earlier the reaction would have been exactly the reverse. Before the discovery of general relativity, the kind of relationship suggested by Blackett would have been shrugged aside as just one more curious numerical coincidence, of which there were so many; while Lord Rayleigh's observations would have been acclaimed at their face value, since they were not strictly incompatible with the theories current at the time regarding the nature of atomic processes.

We can see here the vital function exercised by current beliefs as to the nature of things with respect to the course of scientific development. It may well turn out that scientific opinion has misplaced its beliefs in one, or even in both, of the instances I have given. Yet this would be no reason for refusing to exercise such fiduciary decisions, since without them science could not operate at all.

This has to be borne in mind when we see scientific opinion committing serious errors in suppressing new discoveries, a memorable example of which is offered by the history of hypnotism. The process called to-day "hypnosis" seems to have been known among non-scientific people from the earliest days. The potency of curses among primitive tribes may be due to hypnosis. The practices of Hindu fakirs are other examples of it and many magical performances, as well as some reputed Christian miracles, can now be explained in terms of it.

However, our fundamental beliefs of science first arose in direct opposition to beliefs in sorcery and miracles, and the ancient facts of hypnotism therefore found no place in the new scientific outlook. They were ignored, along with the innumerable superstitions which science had come to supersede. When the facts were once more brought to light by various scientists about two centuries ago, their observations were quietly ignored by science. Then towards the end of the eighteenth century the matter was brought to a head by the public demonstrations of one Friedrich Anton Mesmer, a Viennese medical practitioner, whose hypnotic cures had spread his fame all over Europe. Scientific commissions repeatedly investigated the facts produced by Mesmer and either denied them or explained them away. Finally, Mesmer was broken, his art discredited and he himself stigmatized as an imposter. A generation later another pioneer of hypnotism, Elliotson, a professor of medicine at the University of London, was ordered by the university authorities to discontinue his hypnotic experiments; whereupon he resigned his chair. At about the same time, Esdaile, a surgeon in the service of the Government of India, performed as many as 300 major operations under hypnotic anaesthesia, but medical journals refused to publish his account of these cases. His patients, who had uncomplainingly suffered their limbs to be cut off, were charged with collusion. In England, in 1842, W. S. Ward amputated a thigh with the patient under mesmeric trance and reported the case to the Royal Medical and Chirurgical Society. The evidence indicated that the patient had felt no pain during the operation. The Society, however, refused to believe. Marshall Hall (the pioneer in the study of reflex action) urged that the patient must have been an imposter and the note of the paper having been read was struck from the minutes of the Society. Eight years later, Marshall Hall informed the Society that the patient had confessed to an imposture, but that the source of this information was indirect and confidential. The patient, however, thereupon signed a declaration that the operation had been painless.[3]

The conflict was passionate and violent. Braid, a medical practitioner of Manchester, who took up the matter shortly before Esdaile, was listened to with somewhat lessened hostility, for he started off by attacking the followers of Mesmer and attempting to explain away the process of suggestion. But even Braid's work (which finally did establish the reality of suggestion) was neglected and ignored for another twenty years after his death. It was not until Charcot took up hypnosis at the Salpetrière in Paris, almost a century after Mesmer's acclamation by the lay public, that hypnotism gained full acceptance among scientists.

The hatred against the discoverers of a phenomenon which threatened to undo the cherished beliefs of science

3. This account of Ward's case is given by E. G. Boring, *History of Experimental Psychology*, (1929), p. 120. I have relied on that work also for other parts of the history of Mesmerism.

was as bitter and inexorable as that of the religious persecutors two centuries before. It was, in fact, of the same character.

A contemporary parallel to the disregard of the facts of hypnotism by science would seem to be the present attitude of science to Extra-sensory Perception. I am not concerned here with the question whether this attitude is right or wrong, as I am not sure of it myself. I only want to show here what I mean by scientific beliefs, the holding and applying of which is essential to the pursuit of scientific inquiry.

III

People who accept the findings of science do not usually regard this as a personal act of faith. They think that they are submitting to evidence which by its nature compels their assent and which has the power to compel a similar measure of assent from any rational human being. For modern science is the outcome of a rebellion against all authority. Descartes led the way by his programme of universal doubt: *de omnibus dubitandum*. The Royal Society was founded with the motto: *Nullius in verba*, We accept no authority. Bacon had claimed that science was to be based on purely empirical methods, and *Hypotheses non fingo*, No speculations! echoed Newton. Science has been through the centuries the scourge of all creeds which embodied an act of faith and was supposed—and is commonly still supposed—to be built, in contrast to these creeds, on a foundation of hard facts, and on facts alone.

Yet it is quite easy to see that this is not true, as David Hume first pointed out some 200 years ago. The argument can be stated without any verbal ambiguities in simple mathematical terms. Suppose the evidence on which a scientific proposition is to be based consists of a number of measurements made at various observed times or in coincidence with some other measurable parameter. Let us in other words have pairs of two measured variables, v_1 and v_2. Can we decide from a series of points v_1 plotted against v_2 whether there is a function $v_1 = f(v_2)$ and if so, what it is? Clearly, we can do nothing of the kind. Any set of pairs of v_1 and v_2 values is compatible with an infinite number of functional relations between which there is nothing to choose from the point of view of the underlying data. To choose any of the infinite possible functions and give it the distinction of a scientific proposition is so far without any justification. The measured data are insufficient for the construction of a definite function $v_1 = f(v_2)$ in exactly the same sense as two elements of a triangle are insufficient to determine a definite triangle.

This conclusion is not altered but only obscured by introducing the element of scientific prediction. For one thing, prediction is not a regular attribute of scientific propositions. Kepler's laws and the Darwinian theory predicted nothing. At any rate, successful prediction does not fundamentally change the status of a scientific proposition. It only adds a number of observations, the predicted observations, to our series of measurements and cannot change the fact that any series of measurements is incapable of defining a function between the measured variables.[4]

Since some readers may be reluctant to accept this, I shall illustrate it a little further. Suppose a player of roulette observes the number of colours that have turned up in a hundred consecutive throws. He may plot them in a graph and derive a function in the light of which he will make a prediction. He may try it out and win. He may try it again and win; and win a third time. Would that prove this generalization? No, it would

---

4. This argument was first stated in my *Science, Faith and Society*, (1946), p. 7.

Average Gestation Period and $n\pi$

n	$n\pi$	AVERAGE GESTATION PERIOD (DAYS)	NO. OF PREGNANCIES	ANIMAL
10	31·416	31·41	64	English Rabbit
36	113·097	113·1 ± 0·12	203	Pig
48	150·796	150·8 ± 0·13	195	Karakul Sheep
		150·8 ± 0·19	391	Black Forest Goat
49	153·938	154	?	Saanen Goat
92	289·026	288·9	428	Simmental Cow

only prove that some roulette players are very lucky—i.e. we could consider these predictions to be mere coincidences.

A few years ago there appeared in *Nature*[5] a table of figures proving with great accuracy that the time of gestation, measured in days, of a number of different animals ranging from rabbits to cows is a multiple of the number π. I have reprinted the table here to show how striking is the agreement. Yet an exact relationship of this kind makes no impression on the modern scientist and no amount of further confirmatory evidence would convince him that there is any relation between the period of gestation of animals and multiples of the number π.

Anyone who has friends among astrologers can get from them instances of strikingly fulfilled predictions, which would be hard to rival in science. Yet scientists refuse even to consider the merits of astrological predictions.

In science itself I could tell of predictions which were most strikingly verified and yet were based on premises which later were found to be quite erroneous. Such was the case of the discovery of heavy hydrogen. There is no ratio-

5. *Nature,* Vol. 146, (1940), p. 620.

nal criterion by which the accidental fulfilment of a prediction can be discriminated from its true confirmation.

Those who are convinced that science can be based exclusively on data of experience, have tried to avoid the weight of such critical analysis by reducing the claims of science to a more moderate level. They point out that scientific propositions do not claim to be true, but only to be likely; that they do not predict anything with certainty, but only with probability; that they are provisional and make no claim to finality.

All this is entirely beside the point. If anyone claims that given two angles he can construct the triangle, his claim is equally nonsensical whether he claims to give a true construction or merely a probable construction, or the construction of a merely probable triangle. The selection of one element out of an infinite set of elements all of which satisfy the conditions set by the problems, remains equally unjustifiable whatever positive quality we attach to our selection. Its value is exactly nought. In fact, scientists would object just as much to serial rules in games of chance or astrological predictions, or to relations between times of gestation of animals and the number π, whether these are claimed with certainty, or only with probability, or else merely provisionally. They would be regarded as no less nonsensical for that.

Nor does another attempt to lessen the burden of responsibility on the scientists' shoulders prove more successful. Science, it is said, does not claim to discover the truth but only to give a description or summary of observational data. But why then object to astrology or the description of periods of pregnancy in multiples of the number π? Obviously, because these are not held to be *true* or *rational* descriptions; which brings the problem back exactly to where it was before. For it is no easier to find a justification for picking out one description of the observational data as true or as rational, than it is to pick out any other relationship, whatever its claims may be.

Again, the attempt has been made to lessen the difficulty of justifying the claims of science by suggesting that the statements of science do not claim to be true, except in the sense of being simple. But scientists do not reject astrology, magic or the cosmogony of the Bible because these are not simple enough. That has nothing to do with it. Unless indeed the word "simple" is tortured into meaning "rational," and finally made to coincide with "true."

Whichever way we turn we cannot avoid being faced with the fact that the validity of scientific statements is not compellingly inherent in the evidence to which they refer. Those who believe in science must admit, therefore, that they are placing on the evidence of their senses an interpretation for which they must themselves take a distinct measure of responsibility. In accepting science as a whole and in subscribing to any particular statement of science, they are relying to a certain extent on personal convictions of their own.

IV

The positivist may admit that scientific interpretations include a fiduciary element, but will insist that even so there exists a core of hard facts or incontestable primary sensations, which any theory will have to accept as such.

However, it is very difficult to discover any such primary sensations which are given previous to our interpretation of them.[6] A child presented with a number of objects on a tray will notice only those with which it has some previous familiarity. The Fuegians, whom Charles Darwin visited from the

6. "A pure sensation is an abstraction" says William James in *The Principles of Psychology,* Vol. II, p. 3. This view has since been powerfully developed by Gestalt psychology. My examples illustrating organized perception are mostly taken from the writings of this school.

Beagle, were excited by the sight of the small boats which took the landing party ashore, but failed to notice the ship itself, lying at anchor in front of them.[7] Our eyeballs are full of small floating opaque bodies which we do not normally notice, but which fill us with alarm when some eye trouble calls our attention to them. There is a blind spot in our field of vision which can obliterate a man's head at six feet distance, but seems to have gone unnoticed throughout recorded history until comparatively recent times. To say that we have sensations which we do not notice seems hardly acceptable. But the moment we notice a thing, say by sight, we perceive it *as* something. We usually perceive it as being at some distance and as forming part of something else or standing out against other things as its background. Implicit in these perceptions will be the object's size and its being at rest or in motion. The perceived colour of an object will largely depend on our interpretation of it. A dinner jacket in sunshine is seen as black and snow at dusk is seen as white, though the white snow sends less light into the eye than the black dinner jacket. Such facts as these leave little scope for sensations as primarily given data. They show that even at the most elementary stages of cognition, we are already committing ourselves to an act of interpretation.

There is always a measure of choice in our manner of perception, and whenever we see something in one way we cannot see it at the same time in a different way. A black spot on a white background may be seen either as a blot or as a hole, but the eye must choose between the two ways of seeing it. We may see a passing train at rest and feel ourselves moving, or the reverse, but we must choose between the two forms of perception. An attack on our senses may well compel our attention. But if it does, it will also compel

7. William James, *The Principles of Psychology*, (1891), Vol. II, p. 110.

perception and we shall commit ourselves to some way of receiving the impression and not know it in any other form.

These observations have general significance. When you adopt one way of looking at things you destroy at the same moment some alternative way of seeing them. This is the reason why open controversy is deliberately used as a method of discovering the truth. In a courtroom, for example, counsels for the prosecution and for the defence are each required to take one side of the question at issue. It is supposed that only by committing themselves in opposite directions can they discover all that can be found in favour of each side. If, instead, the judge would enter into friendly consultation with counsel for both sides and seek to establish agreement between them, this would be considered a gross miscarriage of justice.

But it is not often realized that even in the scientific handling of inanimate systems different approaches are possible, which are mutually exclusive. The laws of nature very often make definite predictions. For example Boyle's law, $pv = $ const., is such a prediction of the changes of pressure accompanying the expansion or compression of a gas. Whether or not any particular gas under observation shall be judged to fulfil or falsify this prediction may still require to be decided; but even so the theoretical prediction would be definite. Take, on the other hand, a radioactive atom which is prone to disintegration and of which we know the probable lifetime. Suppose this probable lifetime were an hour. It is quite easy to imagine an apparatus by which we could observe the decomposition of such a single atom and —to avoid irrelevant side issues—we may imagine also that this atom is the only one of its kind in the world. Its probable life-period would clearly predict something about the atom's behaviour, but nothing so definite as $pv = $ const. In accepting it to be true that the probable life-period is an hour we commit ourselves to an expectation, but if it is not fulfilled—

if the atom decomposes after five seconds or keeps us waiting for a week—we can only say that we are surprised; for our affirmation was only of the likelihood of an event and did not exclude the possibility that the unlikely would happen.

The two kinds of expectations which I have just described may be entertained in respect to the same situation, but they are mutually exclusive. We can say that the chance of throwing a double six with two dice is 1:36; but we could not say this, nor anything about the chances of such a throw, if we knew exactly the mechanical conditions prevailing at the moment of the throw. We could predict from these the result of the throw—but the conception of chances would have vanished and would remain inconceivable for a system known in such detail. Thus a more detailed knowledge may completely destroy a pattern which can be envisaged only from a point of view excluding such knowledge.

Something very similar applies to a machine, the detailed observation of which may be wholly irrelevant and therefore misleading. What matters to the understanding of an object as a machine is exclusively the *principle* of its operation. The knowledge of such a principle, as defined for example by a patent, will leave the physical particulars of the machine widely indeterminate. The principle of the lever, for example, can be employed in such an infinite variety of forms, that hardly any physical characteristic could apply to all of them. It represents a logical category, which is in danger of being obscured by a detailed description of an object to which it applies.

Again, there are inanimate objects which function as signs: for example, marks on paper forming the letter "a." These marks, taken as a sign, must not be *observed* but *read.* Observation of a sign as an object destroys its significance as a sign. If you repeat the word "travel" twenty times in succession you become fully aware of the motion of your tongue and the sounds involved in saying "travel," but you dissolve the meaning of the word "travel."

Martin Buber and J. H. Oldham have brought out the fundamental difference between treating a person as a person or as an object. In the former relation we *encounter* the person, in the latter we do not see it as a person at all. Love is a manner of encounter. We may love the same person as a child, as a man or woman and finally in old age; we may continue to love that person after his or her death. Any attempt to fix our relation to a person by the observation of his features or his behaviour is bound to jeopardize therefore our encounter with his person. A man or woman, regarded in their purely physical aspects, may be the object of desire but cannot be truly loved. Their person has been destroyed.

The most important pair of mutually exclusive approaches to the same situation is formed by the alternative interpretations of human affairs in terms of causes and reasons. You can try to represent human actions completely in terms of their natural causes. This is in fact the programme of positivism to which I have referred before. If you carry this out and regard the actions of men, including the expression of their convictions, wholly as a set of responses to a given set of stimuli, then you obliterate any grounds on which the justification of those actions or convictions could be given or disputed. You can interpret, for example, this essay in terms of the *causes* which have determined my action of writing it down or you may ask for my *reasons* for saying what I say. But the two approaches—in terms of causes and reasons—mutually exclude each other.

V

Positivism has made us regard human beliefs as arbitrary personal manifestations, which must be discarded if we are to achieve a proper scientific detachment; belief must be rehabilitated from this discredit if it is to form henceforth a recognized part of our scientific convictions.

Scientific beliefs are not a personal concern. Even though a belief were held by one person alone, as may have been the case for Columbus's belief in a western approach to the Indies when he first conceived it, that does not make it an individual preference—like the love of one's wife and children. The beliefs of scientists concerning the nature of things are held with a claim to universal validity and thus possess normative character. I would describe science, therefore, as a normative belief, which I share; just as astrology is a normative belief which I reject—but which is accepted by astrologers.

Turning now to the contention that beliefs are arbitrary, I shall have to enlarge somewhat on the holding of beliefs in general. Whoever embraces a belief, accepts a commitment. Commitments are regularly entered upon not only by people who believe something, but by almost any living being, and particularly by all animals engaged in purposive (goal-seeking) action. A floating amoeba will emit pseudopods in all directions, until its nucleus is left bare of protoplasm at the centre. When one of the pseudopods touches solid ground, all the others are drawn in and the whole mass of protoplasm is sent flowing towards the new point of anchorage. Such is the amoeba's mode of locomotion. We have here the prototype of a phenomenon which is repeated in a million variants throughout the animal kingdom. There is co-ordination between the simultaneous movements of the animal's limbs and also between movements following upon each other in time. We may characterize such co-ordinated sequences by the fact that any part of the sequence is meaningless by itself, while each makes sense in conjunction with the other parts. Each can be understood only as part of a stratagem for the achievement of a result which, we have reason to believe, gives satisfaction to the animal, e.g. getting food or escaping from danger. The more roundabout are the methods employed in achieving a purpose, the more sagacious will appear their co-ordination and the more clearly will we recognize in them a sustained striving for that purpose.

To say that an action is purposive is to admit that it may miscarry. If it is the purpose of animals to survive until they have reproduced themselves, then surely the vast majority of purposive actions do miscarry; for only a small fraction of each generation of animals lives to beget young. In any case, no animal engaging in a purposive action can be certain that the efforts it is about to make will bear fruit. Nor can there be any certainty that an alternative course of action might not have had a greater chance of success. All purposive action therefore commits its agent to certain risks. Purposive forms of behaviour are a string of irrevocable and uncertain commitments.

Commitments of this kind might be said to express a belief; where there is purposive striving, there is belief in success. Certainly no one can be said truly to believe in anything unless he is prepared to commit himself on the strength of his belief. We conclude that the holding of a belief is a commitment of which human beings are capable, and which bears close analogy to the commitment in which animals universally and quite inevitably engage when embarking on a purposive course of behaviour.

Let us now return to scientific beliefs. When we say that an affirmation of a scientist is true or false, we usually have no need to refer explicitly to our fundamental scientific beliefs. We may turn our backs on them and take them for granted as the unconscious foundation of our judgment. But when some major question is at stake (like hypnotism, telepathy, etc.), our beliefs do become visibly active participants in the controversy, and we find it then more appropriate to say, for example, "I cannot believe this to be true."

Such a belief may turn out to be true or false, as the case may be, but the affirmation of the belief falls into neither of these categories. The affirmation of a belief can only be said to be either *sincere* or *insincere*. Sincere beliefs are those to which we are committed, and a fiduciary commitment is therefore by definition sincere. Our commitments may turn out to have been *rash*. But it is in the nature of a belief that at the moment of its being held it cannot be fully justified, since it is inherent in all commitments that at the time we engage upon them their outcome is still uncertain.

Therefore, the only grounds on which the sincere holding of a belief or the entering on any other kind of commitment can be criticized, is for not having sufficiently taken into consideration its possible rashness. But we must remember that any postponement of judgment for the sake of its reconsideration is itself a commitment. To go on hesitating for the sake of making more certain of one's decision may be the most disastrous, and indeed the most irresponsible, course to choose. So that when a belief is both sincerely and responsibly held—that is, in conscientious awareness of its own conceivable fallibility—there is an affirmation present which cannot be criticized on any grounds whatsoever. It is a form of being, the justification of which cannot be meaningfully questioned.

Such a situation is, of course, subject to revision, and the present moment's belief can be rejected or modified by the next moment's reflection, but this reflection, and its result, will be again an ultimate commitment, which so far cannot have yet become the object of reflection or criticism. Commitment must have duration. Any attempt to accompany it simultaneously by reflection is logically self-contradictory, and, if persisted in, results in the disintegration of our person. If we cannot lose ourselves at all, but feel compelled to observe ourselves in all we do, we become disembodied in the manner which Sartre has penetratingly described. People who cannot rid themselves of the feeling that they are "play-acting" become incapable of holding convictions. The result is not a superior degree of detachment, but an impotent nihilism.

Detachment in the rigorous sense of the word can only be achieved in a state of complete imbecility well below the normal animal's level.[8] In all states of mind above that, we are inevitably committed, and usually we are committed to an approach which excludes other approaches. The descriptive scientific approach as conceived by positivism is inadequate even for the handling of inanimate systems in which we have to assess chances or understand machines, or read signs; and when applied to persons (human or animal) and their actions, it dissolves them both as persons and as rational beings. This approach, far from representing a state of absolute detachment, is in fact a commitment to a set of specific, and as it happens, extremely unreasonable pre-suppositions, to which no one would conceivably commit himself but for the fact that they are taken to provide the one completely detached, objective approach to the world.

Detachment in the ordinary and true sense always means commitment to a particular approach which we deem to be proper to the occasion and disengagement from other points of view which for the time being are inadmissable. To hold the balance between our alternative possible approaches is our ultimate commitment, the most fundamental of all.

8. I am thinking here of the dementia of de-cerebrated dogs (Goltz), decorticated rats (Lashley, *Brain Mechanism and Intelligence*, p. 138), and of the pure reflex behaviour of incomplete lower organisms, such as *Planaria* described by Kepner (*Animals Looking into the Future*, [1925], p. 176). In such cases we observe incoherent behaviour, sustaining no purpose.

VI

The beliefs which men hold are mostly imparted to them by their early education. Some we acquire later through professional training and through the wide variety of educative influences which infiltrate our minds from the press, from works of fiction and through other innumerable contacts. These beliefs form far-reaching systems, and though each of us is directly affected only by one limited part of them, we are committed by implication to the whole pattern of which this is a part.

The transmission of beliefs in society is mostly not by precept, but by example. To take science: there is no textbook which would even attempt to teach how to make discoveries, nor even what evidence should be accepted in science as substantiating a claim to discovery. The whole practice of research and verification is transmitted by example and its standards are upheld by a continuous interplay of criticism within the scientific community. No one who has experienced the woeful unreliability of scientific output coming from places where scientific standards have not been firmly established by tradition, or who has felt the difficulty of doing good scientific work within such a *milieu,* will fail to appreciate the communal character of the premises on which modern scientific work is based.[9]

Scientists are, of course, never unanimous on *all* questions. There may even be clashes from time to time about the general nature of things and the fundamental methods of science (as in the case of hypnotism, telepathy, etc.). Yet the consensus of scientific beliefs has not been seriously endangered during the past 300 years, until the attempt by Soviet Russia to secede from the international community of science and establish a new scientific community, based on

9. This subject is worked out in detail below, p. 68.

markedly different beliefs. Up to then, there had always been between scientists in all parts of the world, and between each generation and the next, sufficient consensus of fundamental beliefs to assure the settlement of all differences.

The scientific community is held together and all its affairs are peacefully managed through its joint acceptance of the same fundamental scientific beliefs. These beliefs, therefore, may be said to form the constitution of the scientific community and to embody its ultimate sovereign general will. The freedom of science consists in the right to pursue the exploration of these beliefs and to uphold under their guidance the standards of the scientific community. For this purpose a measure of self-government is required, by virtue of which scientists will maintain a framework of institutions, granting independent positions to mature scientists; the candidates for these posts being selected under the direction of scientific opinion. Such is the autonomy of science in the West, which logically flows from the nature of the basic purpose and the fundamental beliefs, to which the community of scientists is dedicated here.

The Marxist conception of science is different from that of the West, and its application in Russia has already led to serious changes in the position of science there and to a breach, at various points, between the scientific opinions of East and West. The most far-reaching action in this direction was the official and sweeping repudiation of Mendel's laws, and of the whole conception of biology related to these laws, by the Soviet Academy on the 26th August, 1948.

There was much indignant protest in Britain against this decision of the Soviet Academy and even more against the pressure exercised by the Soviet Government, to which the Russian Academy had yielded in taking this action. I subscribe to these protests, but I wish their proper theoretical foundation were more clearly realized. If you protest in the name of freedom in general, it is embarrassing to admit that hitherto it was the Anti-Mendelists and the whole school of Michurin and Lysenko, whose publications were excluded from all the leading scientific journals of Soviet Russia and whose teachings were unrepresented in Russian university curricula; as they of course continue to be in the West. Marxians were quite right in pointing out that there always exist accepted views on certain general issues which are imposed by scientific opinion on scientific journals, textbooks and academic curricula, and from which candidates for scientific posts will dissent at great peril to their future chances. They were right also in recalling that the views thus imposed were sometimes found later to be untrue and the dissenters vindicated.

We must admit that the existing body of science—or at any rate its fundamental beliefs—is an orthodoxy in the West. Millions are spent annually on the cultivation and dissemination of science by the public authorities, who could not give a penny for the advancement of astrology or sorcery. In other words, our civilization is deeply committed to certain beliefs about the nature of things; beliefs which are different, for example, from those to which the early Egyptian or the Aztec civilizations were committed. It is for the cultivation of these particular beliefs—and these alone —that a certain group of people has been granted a measure of independence and official support in the West.

This is what we call academic freedom. Replace science as we know it, by some other study we do not believe in and we cease to protest against political interference with its pursuit. Suppose, for example, that Lysenko and his supporters were given a clean thirty years to transform biology, physics and chemistry in the image of dialectical materialism throughout the universities of the U.S.S.R.; and that subsequently, by some miracle, Marxism were abandoned by the

Government of the Soviet Union. We would certainly not uphold the academic liberties of the then occupants of scientific positions against an Anti-Lysenko acting as Lysenko does to-day, but this time for the re-establishment of our conception of science. We may demand a measure of freedom for almost any nonsense in a free country, but that is not what we mean by academic freedom.

Those who engage with Marxists in discussion about the freedom of science must face up to this situation. The Marxists are quite near the truth in saying that in demanding freedom we merely seek to establish our own orthodoxy. The only valid objection to this is that our fundamental beliefs are not just an orthodoxy; they are true beliefs which we are prepared to uphold. This true vision also happens to open greater scope for freedom than other, false visions; that is so, but in any case, our commitment to what we believe to be true comes first.

More generally, the freedom of science cannot be defended to-day on the basis of a positivist conception of science, which involves a positivist programme for the ordering of society. The true fulfilment of such a programme is the destruction of the free society and the establishment of totalitarianism.

For a complete causal interpretation of man and human affairs disintegrates all rational grounds on which man can hold convictions and act on these convictions. It leaves you with a picture of human affairs construed in terms of appetites, checked only by fear. All you have to explain then in order to understand history, and with it politics, law, science, music, etc., is why at certain moments the appetite of one group gets the upper hand over its rivals. You have various options at this point; Marx and Engels decided to answer the question in terms of class war. They affirmed that the class which, by taking control of the means of production can make best use of them for the production of wealth, will prevail. The victory of the rising class is inevitable, though it can be achieved only by violence; for no ruling class can agree to its own annihilation. This theory was put forward as a scientific proposition: as the discovery of the "laws of motion" governing society. And indeed some conception of this kind does inevitably follow from a consistent application of the positivist programme to the affairs of man.

According to the positivist theory of society, no human judgment—be it in politics, law or art, or any other field of human thought, including science itself—can be said to be valid except in the sense that it serves the interests of a certain power. In the Marxist version this is the power of the rising class, and to-day in particular the power of the vanguard of the rising class, as embodied in the Soviet Government. That is the theory of science facing us in Russia to-day. Here the positivist movement, which had set out to establish the reign of science over all human thought, is culminating in the overthrow of science itself.

The free society—of which a free scientific community naturally forms part—can be defended only by expressly recognizing the characteristic beliefs which are held in common by such a society and professing that these beliefs are true. The principal belief—or I should rather say the main truth—underlying a free society, is that man is amenable to reason and susceptible to the claims of his conscience. By reason are meant here such things as the ordinary practice of objectivity in establishing facts and of fairness in passing judgment in individual cases. The citizens of a free society believe that by such methods they will be able to resolve jointly—to the sufficient satisfaction of all—whatever dissension may exist among them to-day or may arise in the future. They see an inexhaustible scope for the better adjustment of social institutions and are resolved to achieve this peacefully, by agreement.

Just as on a smaller scale the scientific community organizes, disciplines and defends the cultivation of certain beliefs held by its members, so the free society as a whole is sustained for the practice and by the practice of certain wider, but still quite distinctive, beliefs. The ideal of a free society is in the first place to be a *good* society; a body of men who respect truth, desire justice and love their fellows.[10] It is only because these aspirations coincide with the claims of our own conscience, that the institutions which secure their pursuit are recognized by us as the safeguards of our freedom. It is misleading to describe a society thus constituted, which is an instrument of our consciences, as established for the sake of our individual selves; for it protects our conscience from our own greed, ambition, etc., as much as it protects it against corruption by others. Morally, men live by what they sacrifice to their conscience; therefore the citizen of a free society, much of whose moral life is organized through his civic contacts, largely depends on society for his moral existence. His social responsibilities give him occasion to a moral life from which men not living in freedom are debarred. That is why the free society is a true end in itself, which may rightly demand the services of its members in upholding its institutions and defending them.

10. Note added in December 1949: Churchill has often said that affection between Englishmen is the safeguard of their freedom. A recent instance was his reply in Parliament to Mr. Attlee's birthday greetings (1.12.49). These, he said, brought home to him "how far more great are all those sentiments which united us than are the still quite important matters which are so often the occasion of debate in this house and out of doors." Compare the precarious hold of free institutions in Germany, owing to lack of friendly sentiments among political opponents; as manifested—also quite recently—by the leader of the Opposition accusing the German Chancellor of serving the Allies.

The fiduciary formulation and acceptance of science fits in with our fiduciary conception of the free society. Scientific beliefs are a part of the beliefs cultivated in such a society and accepted by its members. That is their valid defence against Marxism. But we must realize that this defence accepts a position for knowledge in society which in many ways recalls that assigned to it by Marxism. It implies that the free society upholds an orthodoxy which excludes certain suppositions that are widely current to-day. Any representation of man and of the affairs of man, which, if consistently upheld, would destroy the constitutive beliefs of a free society must be denied by this orthodoxy. A behaviourism which denies the very existence of the moral sphere for the sake of which the free society is constituted, or a psychology which discredits as mere secondary rationalization the purposes which a free society regards as its mainsprings, will be rejected by this orthodoxy.

The free society would cease to exist if its members ever admitted that some major conflict will have to be settled by sheer force within the society. Such an admission would therefore be subversive of the free society and constitute an act of disloyalty to it. Nor should members of a free society ever admit that experience can disprove that moral forces operate in history, any more than a scientist will admit that experience can disprove the scientific conception of the nature of things. They should persist, on the contrary, in searching history for the manifestation of a sense of justice, and try to discover in every reconciliation and pacification the fruits of human confidence, responding to confidence.

Science or scholarship can never be more than an affirmation of the things we believe in. These beliefs will, by their very nature, be of a normative character, claiming universal validity; they must also be responsible beliefs, held in due consideration of evidence and of the fallibility of all beliefs; but eventually they are ultimate commitments, issued under the seal of our personal judgment. To all further critical scruples we must at some point finally reply: "For I believe so."

We are living in the midst of a period requiring great readjustments. One of these is to learn once more to hold beliefs, our own beliefs. The task is formidable, for we have been taught for centuries to hold as a belief only the residue which no doubt can conceivably assail. There is no such residue left to-day, and that is why the ability to believe with open eyes must once more be systematically re-acquired.

3

Foundations of Academic Freedom[1]

The analysis of the grounds on which freedom rests is of great practical interest to those who value freedom. For by clarifying these grounds we may hope to make them more secure. By raising questions concerning the nature and justification of freedom, we may try to eliminate some of its ambiguities which have, particularly in our days, laid freedom open to misunderstanding, and worse, to perversion and discredit.

Freedom is ambiguous for there are different ways of being free. One way is to be free from external constraint. The rational limits to this freedom are set by the condition that it must not interfere with other people's right to the same freedom. I have, for example, freedom to choose between going to sleep or listening to the wireless, so long as my listening does not interfere with my neighbour's choice between the same two alternatives. This is the approach to freedom which the great utilitarians have impressed on our age. It is linked to the idea that the basic pursuit of a good

1. *The Lancet*, 1947.

society is the greatest happiness of its greatest number and that freedom is a condition of this pursuit. This individualist or self-assertive conception of freedom can, unfortunately, be used to justify all kinds of objectionable behaviour. At some time or other it has been invoked in protection of the worst forms of exploitation, including even the keeping of slaves. It has served as the ground for the Romantic Movement in its exaltation of the unique, lawless individual and of nations striving for greatness at any price. Its fundamental opposition to all restraint can easily be turned into nihilism.

Another conception of freedom is in its extreme form almost the opposite of the first. It regards freedom as liberation from personal ends by submission to impersonal obligations. Its prototype is Luther facing the hostile Assembly at Worms with the words, "Hier stehe ich und kann nicht anders." Such surrender to moral compulsion is certainly a form of liberation. But the theory of such freedom can become very much like a theory of totalitarianism. It does become altogether totalitarian if you regard the State as the supreme guardian of the public good; for it then follows that the individual is made free by surrendering completely to the State.

These discrepancies in the conception of freedom are a real danger to it. For even without considering the extremes either of nihilism or totalitarianism, we may well feel that the individualist theory of freedom is selfish or at least uninspiring, while the theory of freedom by self-surrender does not seem to accord with our sympathy for the individual pursuing his own happiness in his own personal manner.

It seems to me that the study of academic freedom may well serve as a guide in this dilemma. For in the foundations of academic freedom we shall find the two rival aspects of liberty so firmly interwoven that their essential relationship and true balance become easily apparent.

II

The study of academic freedom has at any rate the great advantage that it is fairly easy to say in this case what we mean by freedom. Academic freedom consists in the right to choose one's own problem for investigation, to conduct research free from any outside control, and to teach one's subject in the light of one's own opinions.

At first sight this kind of freedom may seem to raise difficulties for both of the two great theories of freedom. For clearly, the scholar is not given freedom primarily in order to promote his happiness; but neither is he meant merely to fulfil an obligation. While these are both true functions of freedom, some principle seems yet missing which should join the two together—a stereoscope is wanted to unite these two images of freedom. We shall find this by observing yet a third function of it which has hitherto been given little notice in the major philosophic discussions on freedom.

The existing practice of scientific life embodies the claim that freedom is an efficient form of organization. The opportunity granted to mature scientists to choose and pursue their own problems is supposed to result in the best utilization of the joint efforts of all scientists in a common task. In other words: if the scientists of the world are viewed as a team setting out to explore the existing openings for discovery, it is assumed that their efforts will be efficiently co-ordinated if only each is left to follow his own inclinations. It is claimed in fact that there is no other efficient way of organizing the team, and that any attempt to co-ordinate their efforts by directives of a superior authority would inevitably destroy the effectiveness of their co-operation.

Now this, in a way, is surprising. For usually one thinks of co-ordination as a process imposing restraint on the discretionary powers of individuals. Let us try to analyse therefore how it can be true that the opposite holds in science; optimum co-ordination being achieved here by releasing individual impulses.

The usual thing is, of course, that when a number of persons apply themselves independently to parts of the same task, their efforts remain essentially unco-ordinated. A party of women shelling peas represents no co-ordinated effort, for their total achievement is simply the sum of their individual outputs. Similarly, a team of chess players is essentially unco-ordinated; for each plays his opponent according to his own lights and the performance of the team is simply the sum of the games independently won by each member.

By contrast we can see the distinctive character of science coming into view; it is not conducted by isolated efforts like those of the chess players or shellers of peas and could make no progress that way. If one day all communications were cut between scientists, that day science would practically come to a standstill. Discoveries might continue to be made during the first few years of such a regime at about the normal rate, but their flow would soon dry up and henceforth progress would become fitful and sporadic, and the continued systematic growth of science would cease entirely. The co-ordinative principle of science thus stands out in all its simple and obvious nature. It consists in the adjustment of each scientist's activities to the results hitherto achieved by others. In adjusting himself to the others each scientist acts independently, yet by virtue of these several adjustments scientists keep extending together with a maximum efficiency the achievements of science as a whole. At each step a scientist will select from the results obtained by others those elements which he can use best for his own task and will thus make the best possible contribution to science; opening thereby the field for other scientists to make their optimum contribution in their turn—and so on indefinitely.

We are faced here—it would seem—with a basic principle, leading quite generally to co-ordination of individual activities without the intervention of any co-ordinating authority. It is a simple principle of logic which can be demonstrated by quite trivial examples. Suppose, for example, we had to piece together a very large jigsaw puzzle which it would take one person several days or even weeks to complete. And imagine that the matter were really urgent, the discovery of some important secret being dependent on the solution. We would no doubt engage a team of helpers; but how would we organize them? There would be no purpose in farming out a number of sets of the puzzle (which could be duplicated photographically) to several isolated collaborators and then adding up their results after a specified period. Though this method would allow the enlistment of an indefinite number of helpers, it would bear no appreciable results. The only way to get the job finished quickly would be to get as many helpers as could conveniently work at one and the same set and let them loose on it, each to follow his own initiative. Each helper would then watch the situation as it was affected by the progress made by all the others and would set himself new problems in accordance with the latest outline of the completed part of the puzzle. The tasks undertaken by each would closely dovetail into those performed by the others. And consequently the joint efforts of all would form a closely organized whole, even though each helper would follow entirely his own independent judgment.

Moreover, it is obvious what would happen if someone believing in the paramount effectiveness of central direction, were to intervene and try to improve matters by applying the methods of central administration. It is impossible to plan in advance the steps by which a jigsaw puzzle is to be put together. All that a centralized administration could achieve, therefore, would be to form all helpers into a hierarchical body and direct their activities henceforth from one centre. Each would then have to wait for directions from his superior and all would have to wait until a decision is taken at the supreme level. In effect, all participants except the one acting as the head of the organization would cease to make any appreciable contribution to the piecing together of the puzzle. The effect of co-operation would fall to zero.

We can thus see confirmed here the twofold claim that on the one hand the actions of individuals acting according to their own judgment may become spontaneously—and yet efficiently—co-ordinated to a joint task, while on the other hand subordination of the individual efforts to a central authority would destroy their co-ordination. Moreover, we can see clearly adumbrated the applicability of this logic to the self-co-ordination of scientists in the pursuit of discovery. For this logic seems to consist simply in the extension of an unknown pattern by individual steps, under the twofold condition that each suggested new step can be readily judged as to its correctness or otherwise, and that each new step is rapidly brought to the notice of all participants and taken into account by them when they make their own next move.

III

Is this then all that can be said about the curious claim that the avenues of potential discovery are most effectively explored if we let scientists choose their own problems? Is it as simple as that?

In a way it is. The logical basis for the spontaneous co-ordination of scientists in the pursuit of science is as simple as, and in fact identical with, that which operates the self-co-ordination of a team engaged in piecing together a jigsaw puzzle. But there is something profoundly different, and also highly significant, in the way in which the elements of the same logical machinery are provided in either case. For the pieces of a jigsaw puzzle are bought in a shop with the certainty that they will yield a solution known to the manufacturer. But there is no similar assurance given to us by the Creator of our Universe that we shall find an intelligible ground-plan of it by continuing to piece together the elements of our experience.

It is not even clear in what sense science—or scholarship in general, to which all these considerations also apply—can be said to have any comprehensive task at all. The search for a "ground-plan" of the Universe can only be meant in a vague and fluid sense. Pythagoras and even Kepler were seeking a ground-plan in terms of numerical and geometrical rules, Galileo and Newton sought it in terms of mechanism, to-day we are seeking it once more in terms of mathematical harmonies, but other than the number rules of Pythagoras. In the field of general scholarship even more radical changes continue to occur in the purpose of inquiry. Compare the moral interpretation of history by a Lord Acton or a Toynbee with the way history is interpreted by Marxists like Laski and G. D. H. Cole, or by psychoanalysts like Franz Alexander or Jung. Moreover, while in the case of the jigsaw puzzle a new piece either fits into a particular gap or fails to fit into it in the most obvious fashion, in science this is not so. Some new discoveries may click immediately into an indisputable position, but other claims, often more important, remain uncertain for a number of years. To every step of scientific progress there is attached an element of uncertainty regarding its scope and scientific value.

It is unmistakable that the logic of self-co-ordination is based in the case of science, and of scholarship in general, on elements which are much vaguer than those present in the case of a jigsaw puzzle. In science and scholarship the uncertainty of the final task and the dubitability of each single step are indeed such that this may well call in question the whole analogy which we have hitherto pursued.

Yet in my view this is only to be taken as a warning to use this analogy carefully. Take once more the case of science. In spite of the profound changes in general outlook and method which have occurred only in the last 400 years of scientific development, we can see a distinct coherence of the contribution to science during that period. Most of the scientists who were highly respected in their own time are still in high regard among scientists to-day, and few have been added to the ranks of great scientists to-day whose works were generally thought valueless in their own days. It is true that many of Kepler's, or even Galileo's or Newton's arguments may appear irrelevant to-day. And again, Galileo and Newton would probably be profoundly unsatisfied with the kind of explanation quantum mechanics gives us of atomic processes. But Galileo and Newton remain nevertheless classics of modern science. Their discoveries are the very foundations of the picture which we are forming of nature to-day and their methods of investigation are still among the archetypes of the modern scientific method. Their personal example is recognized with unchanging loyalty and indeed with a reverence which increases through the centuries as the realm of science, which they founded, continues to extend its domain.

This coherence of science over the centuries is paralleled by its coherence over all regions of the planet. Some energetic attempts have been made in the past fifteen years or so to make scientists in Germany believe that as Germans they must disbelieve relativity and quantum mechanics, and since 1939 great pressure has been exercised on scientists in Russia to reject Mendelism on account of its supposed incompatibility with Marxism, but these objectionable efforts have happily been sporadic. On the whole, science is still accepted to-day in the same way all over the world.

Here, I believe, we have before us a sufficient logical ground for the spontaneous co-ordination of individual scientific discoveries. The ground is provided by such coherence as science does possess. Insofar as there exists a steady underlying purpose in each step of scientific discovery, and each such step can be competently judged as to its conformity to this purpose and its success in approaching it, these steps can be made to add up spontaneously to the most efficient pursuit of science.

IV

Let us expound this a little further, for it contains the essential result of our whole line of thought.

It is not quite enough to recognize science as pursuing a consistent purpose. So did, in a way, the students of the caballa, the witch hunters and the astrologers, and we must distinguish the purpose of science from that of these erroneous pursuits. We could not speak of a true spontaneous growth of science if we considered the apparent coherence of science as a result of a series of accidents, or as the expression of a persistent error. We must believe on the contrary that it represents the consistent expansion of some kind of truth. In other words we must accept science as something real, as a spiritual reality partly disclosed at any particular moment by the past achievements of science and to be disclosed ever further by discoveries yet to come. We should regard the minds of scientists engaged in research as seeking intuitive contact with these as yet undisclosed parts of science, and look upon discovery as the result of a successful contact with a hitherto hidden reality. Whenever a scientist wrestles with his intellectual conscience, whether to accept or reject an idea, he should be taken to be making contact with the whole tradition of science, in fact with all scientists of the past whose example he is following, all those living whose approval he is seeking and all those yet to come for whom he is proposing to establish a new teaching.

The coherence of science must be regarded as an expression of the common rootedness of scientists in the same spiritual reality. Then only can we properly understand that at every step, each is pursuing a common underlying purpose and that each can sufficiently judge—in general accordance with other scientific opinion—whether his contribution is valid or not. Only then are the conditions for the spontaneous co-ordination of scientists properly established.

This view of the coherence of science leads us back to the two rival aspects of freedom and allows us to combine the two. Science, we can see now, shows strong features corresponding to both aspects of freedom. The assertion of his personal passion is the mark of the great pioneer, who is the salt of the earth in science. Originality is the principal virtue of a scientist and the revolutionary character of scientific progress is indeed proverbial. At the same time science has a most closely knit professional tradition; it rivals the Church of Rome and the legal profession in continuity of doctrine and strength of corporate spirit. Scientific rigour is as proverbial as scientific radicalism. Science fosters a maximum of originality while imposing also an exceptional degree of critical rigour.

And yet between these two aspects there is no disharmony. A clash may occasionally occur between originality of the individual and the critical opinion of his fellow scientists, but there can be no conflict between the *principles* of spontaneity and constraint. There are no romantic scientists who demand the prerogative to express their individuality as such, heedless of other scientists' opinions. The revolutionary in science does not claim to be heard on the grounds of any right to assert his personality against outside compulsion, but because he believes he has grounds for establishing

48

a new universally compelling opinion. He breaks the law as it is, in the name of the law as he believes it ought to be. He has an intensely personal vision of something which in his view henceforth everyone must recognize.

This unity between personal creative passion and willingness to submit to tradition and discipline is a necessary consequence of the spiritual reality of science. When the scientist's intuition seeks discovery, it is reaching out for contact with a reality in which all other scientists participate with him. Therefore, his most personal acts of intuition and conscience link him firmly to the universal system and the canons of science. While the whole progress of science is due to the force of individual impulses, these impulses are not respected in science as such, but only insofar as they are dedicated to the tradition of science and are disciplined by the standards of science.

These considerations can be readily extended to scholarship in general. Academic freedom can claim to be an efficient form of organization for discovery in all fields of systematic study controlled by a tradition of intellectual discipline.

V

The example of the jigsaw puzzle has proved useful. It has guided us to an effective union of the two rival aspects of freedom. This example gave us also a hint concerning the dangers of an outside central authority superseding the impulses of individual initiatives. We can now see more clearly how this applies to academic pursuits, particularly in their relation to the State. If the spontaneous growth of scholarship requires that scholars be dedicated to the service of a transcendent reality, then this implies that they must be free from all temporal authority. Any intervention on the part of an outside authority could only destroy their contact with the aims which they are pledged to pursue.

So far the position is fairly simple. But tolerance of academic freedom by the State is not enough to-day. On the modern scale, institutions of higher learning and higher education can be upheld only by public subsidies. But if scholars are rewarded by the State and given by the State the means for conducting their researches, the government may well bring to bear on them a pressure deflecting them from academic interests and standards. For example, a dairy-producing State, like Iowa, may dislike it if its scholars discover and make known the nutritive and economic advantages of margarine, and the legislature of the State may want to intervene against its own State University to prevent it from publishing such conclusions, as this in fact happened quite recently in Iowa. There are many opportunities for such conflicts between the immediate interests of the State and the interests of learning and truth cultivated for their own sake. How can these conflicts be avoided?

Up to a point the solution to such conflicts is fairly straightforward. The fact that the King appoints and pays the judges does not affect their independence so long as the King is under the law. The King of England also appoints and pays the chief opponent of his own government in the person of the leader of the parliamentary opposition. Governmental patronage is no danger to the independence of the persons appointed, so long as these are allowed to function properly. It then merely amounts to an undertaking by the government to provide fuel and oil for a machine, the operation of which is not controlled by it. In the case of legal appointments, the machine is controlled by the principles of justice as laid down by law and interpreted by the legal profession; while in the case of political appointments, the King sanctions the popular will as expressed through the established electoral machinery.

These examples, particularly that of the appointment of judges by the government, are a close illustration of the way in which the State can give support to academic scholarship, without impairing academic independence. It must regard an independent academic life in the same light as it regards an independent administration of justice. Its respect for scholarship and for the principles guiding the free advancement and dissemination of knowledge must be rooted as deeply as its respect for law and justice. Both should derive validity from similar sources; from transcendent principles embodied in great traditions to the service of which our civilization is dedicated.

But however great the respect of the State for an independent judiciary, it could not give effect to this attitude if the legal profession were divided into rival schools of thought; for the State would then have to arbitrate between these. Something similar holds in respect to scholarship. A government can fully observe the freedom of science in all questions on which scientific opinion has on the whole agreed; but if academic opinion were sharply divided in assessing the merits of discoveries and the abilities of scholars, then there would be no possibility of maintaining academic freedom. Suppose that when the appropriate academic committee assembles to elect a new professor, it could turn for advice to no accepted leaders of scholarship and would have no accepted standards of scholarship by which to judge candidates. Chairs would then have to be filled by the light of other than academic considerations, and the next best thing might probably be to please popular opinion or the government in power. A strong and homogeneous academic opinion, deriving its coherence from its common rootedness in the same scholarly tradition, is an indispensable safeguard of academic freedom. If there exists such an academic opinion, and if popular opinion respects academic opinion, then there is no danger to academic freedom. Then it matters little whether the universities get their money from public or private sources.

A survey of the universities in various countries shows a great variety of machinery for making academic appointments. But I can find very little connection between the nature of these constitutions and the strength of academic freedom established under their dominion. In some Continental countries—e.g. Holland, Belgium, Sweden, Norway, Denmark, Switzerland—State-run universities have been a complete success; whereas in some States of America, for example, they have been repeatedly impaired by an intolerant legislature. The difference lies entirely in the condition of public opinion, which has shown a greater respect for the autonomy of scholarship, say, in the canton of Zürich than in the State of Iowa. Nor is self-government of universities a safeguard against corruption of academic freedom. I know of instances where universities were run for a generation by a clique of professors, keeping up a close system of nepotism and political patronage. Any candidate who had acquired a scientific reputation was regarded as a seeker of publicity who was trying to force himself on the university by unfair practices. While institutional safeguards of academic freedom are desirable, we must not forget that they are not enough, and may even become the shield of a corrupt academic opinion.

Among the desirable institutional safeguards I should like particularly to mention the custom of permanent academic appointments. Appointment for life, or until the age of retirement, grants a high degree of independence to the scholar, as it does to the judge and to the minister of religion. The case of the permanently appointed scholar is, however, somewhat peculiar. For in contrast to the judge and the minister, his obligations are not even remotely laid down by any explicit rule. His duties as teacher and administrator should not take up all his time, but leave him free to devote his principal energies to creative work. There is no way of enforcing that he will go on doing such work. All you can rely on is his love of his work and the hope that this love will last. You cannot expect that love to be replaced by a sense of duty, as it may perhaps be in marriage; for no one can make discoveries from a sense of duty without creative passion. We can see here how completely the personal aspect of freedom—the liberty to assert oneself—coincides in the field of scholarship with the social aspect of freedom, which is a surrender to the service of impersonal principles.

VI

We may like to test these views further by applying them to some questions of detail. We may turn for example to the difference, which at first sight appears puzzling, between the independent standing claimed here for members of the academic profession and the admittedly subordinate condition of well-trained scientists engaged in various forms of surveying and of scholars employed as bibliographers and the like. This difference finds its ready justification in the distinction between creative and routine work. We may recall the example of the jigsaw puzzle. The helpers are granted individual liberty because they have to guess their way at each step. To guess the solution to a problem offered by nature—as demanded of the scientist—requires the exercise of intuitive faculties controlled by an intellectual conscience. They are the means for establishing creative contacts with a hidden reality. Each such contact will lead to a new departure in a more or less unexpected direction, and it is precisely in order to find these directions that each scholar is made to act independently. In a process of surveying, on the other hand, the direction of progress is necessarily laid down in advance. Surveying entails therefore that the helpers engaged in it should accept a comprehensive project laid down for them beforehand. When such a scheme is in existence, its fulfilment by the contributions of the individual surveyors can be directed by a central authority, and it is desirable that it should be so directed. The tasks of individual surveyors will be quite properly allocated to them from above; they have no claim to academic freedom.

It is equally easy to dispose of the claim to academic freedom of applied scientists in industry or government offices. There is a good deal of confusion, intellectual, emotional and political, on this subject. The obvious fact of the matter is that any research which is conducted explicitly for a purpose other than that of the advancement of knowledge, must be guided ultimately by the authorities responsible for that outside purpose. Such external purposes are usually practical, like the waging of war, or the improvement of some public service—like telephones or roads—or simply the earning of profits for a firm operating in industry. If the research worker is to serve any of these purposes he must submit his own contribution to the judgment of those who are ultimately responsible for waging war, running the telephone system, building roads, or making profits for a commercial enterprise. He must accept their decision as to what is required of him for their purposes. He will do his job well only, if after due discussion, he relies confidently on the final decision of the chief executive to whom he is responsible. The degree of subordination essential to the successful working of the applied scientist will vary a great deal. But there should be no difficulty in dealing with any particular case on the basis of the same general principle. Broadly speaking, you must choose between dedication to the advancement of a system of knowledge which requires freedom, or the pursuit of applied science which involves subordination.

There is of course no difference in the personal respect due to the individual engaged in surveying or in applied science, as compared with the respect due to a pure scientist. He may be the same man at different periods of his life. During the war a large number of academic scientists volunteered to do practical work. They all had to accept a measure of subordination. I merely say that certain jobs require for their efficient performance that men should be free, while others require that they should be subject to direction from above.

VII

Academic freedom is of course never an isolated phenomenon. It can exist only in a free society; for the principles underlying it are the same on which the most essential liberties of society as a whole are founded.

Our analysis of free academic activities has given us a clear conception of men and women evaluating hidden possibilities of the mind. We have observed them living in a common creative tradition and making contact with a spiritual reality underlying that tradition. We have seen them exercising their powers of intuition and judging their own ideas in the light of their intellectual conscience. Reference has been made to important analogies such as the functions of judges and of ministers of religion. These could be readily extended further. In a courtroom, for example, there are others apart from the judges who act on spiritual grounds. There are witnesses who may find it hard to tell the truth and yet do so. There are jurymen and counsel who must try to be fair and who may have occasion to wrestle with their consciences. (Think of the jurymen in the famous trial of Emile Zola, who were harassed by threatening letters and demonstrations at their homes throughout the proceedings.) Everywhere in the world there are people who are trusted by their fellow-men to tell the truth or to be fair; there are consciences touched by compassion, struggling against the ties of comfort or the callousness born of harsh custom.

Our lives are full of such conflicts. Wherever these contacts are made with spiritual obligations, there is an opportunity for asserting liberty. There are great examples in history and there are many small instances every day, of people who assert their liberty on grounds of this kind. A nation whose citizens are sensitive to the claims of conscience and are not afraid to follow them, is a free nation. A country in which questions of conscience are generally regarded as real, and where people are on the whole prepared to admit them as legitimate motives and even to put up with considerable inconvenience or hardship, caused by others acting on such motives—such a country is a free country.

These contacts with transcendent obligations may reach high levels of creativity. They may inspire prophetic announcements or other great innovations. In some fields —as in science, in scholarship or the administration of the law—this will contribute to the development of an intellectual system. In this case we can observe a process of definite self-co-ordination. But all contacts with spiritual reality have a measure of coherence. A free people, among whom many are on the alert for calls on their consciences, will show a spontaneous coherence of this kind. They may feel that it all comes from being rooted in the same national tradition; but this tradition may well be merely a national variant of a universal human tradition. For a similar coherence will be found between different nations when each follows a national tradition of this type. They will form a community of free peoples. They may argue and quarrel, yet will always settle each new difficulty in the end, firmly rooted in the same transcendent ground.

VIII

Finally, let me return briefly to the great problem of the totalitarian danger at which I have hinted at the start. We can see two points emerging from our discussion of academic freedom and of freedom in general.

It appears, first, that the usual antithesis of the individual versus the State is a false guide to the issue of freedom versus totalitarianism. The most essential freedoms, at any rate, are those in which it is not the individual pursuing his personal interests who claims to be respected by the State. Freedom is demanded by the dedicated individual in view of the grounds to which he is dedicated. He speaks to the State as a liegeman of a higher master demanding homage to his master. The true antithesis is therefore between the State and the invisible things which guide men's creative impulses and in which men's consciences are naturally rooted. The general foundations of coherence and freedom in society may be regarded as secure to the extent to which men uphold their belief in the reality of truth, justice, charity and tolerance, and accept dedication to the service of these realities; while society may be expected to disintegrate and fall into servitude when men deny, explain away, or simply disregard these realities and transcendent obligations.

The totalitarian form of the State arises logically from the denial of reality to this realm of transcendent ideas. When the spiritual foundations of all freely dedicated human activities—of the cultivation of science and scholarship, of the vindication of justice, of the profession of religion, of the pursuit of free art and free political discussion

—when the transcendent grounds of all these free activities are summarily denied, then the State becomes, of necessity, inheritor to all ultimate devotion of men. For if truth is not real and absolute, then it may seem proper that the public authorities should decide what should be called the truth. And if justice is not real and absolute, then it may seem proper that the government should decide what shall be considered just or unjust. Indeed, if our conceptions of truth and justice are determined by interests of some kind or other, then it is right that the public interest should over-rule all personal interests in this matter. We have here a full justification of totalitarian statehood.

In other words, while a radical denial of absolute obliga-tions cannot destroy the moral passions of man, it can render them homeless. The desire for justice and brotherhood can then no more confess itself for what it is, but will seek embodi-ment in some theory of salvation through violence. Thus we see arising those sceptical, hardboiled, allegedly scientific forms of fanaticism which are so characteristic of our modern age.

The study of academic freedom which we have pursued may serve to show what is the decisive point in the issue of liberty. It consists in certain metaphysical assumptions with-out which freedom is logically untenable, and without the firm profession of which freedom can be upheld only in a state of suspended logic, which threatens to collapse at any moment and which in these searching and revolutionary times cannot fail to collapse before long.

Man's rapidly increasing destructive powers will soon put the ideas of our time to a crucial test. We may be faced with the fact that only by resuming the great tradition which embodies faith in these realities can the continuance of the human race on earth, equipped with the powers of modern science, be made both possible and desirable.

4

Self-Government
of Science[1]

It is difficult to trace a complete and authoritative statement of the argument used in support of the State control of science; but I believe that in its most precise form it would run as follows. "No scientific statement is absolutely valid, for there are always some underlying assumptions present, the acceptance of which represents an arbitrary act of faith. Arbitrariness prevails once more when scientists choose to pursue research in any one direction rather than another. Since the contents of science and the progress of science both vitally concern the community as a whole, it is wrong to allow decisions affecting science to be taken by private individuals. Decisions such as these should be reserved to the public authorities who are responsible for the public good; whence it follows that both the teaching of science and the conduct of research must be controlled by the State."

I believe this reasoning to be fallacious and its conclusions to be wrong. Yet I shall not try to meet the argu-

1. Address to the Manchester Literary and Philosophical Society, February, 1942.

ment point by point, but will instead oppose it as a whole by analysing the actual state of affairs which it altogether misrepresents. I shall survey the individuals and groups who normally take the decisions which contribute to the growth and dissemination of science. I shall show that the individual scientist, the body of scientists and the general public, each play their part and that this distribution of functions is inherent in the process of scientific development, so that none of these functions can be delegated to a superior authority. I shall argue that any attempt to do this could only result in the distortion—and if persisted in, in the complete destruction—of science. I shall demonstrate instances where such attempts have actually been made and where that destruction actually came to pass.

I

The primary decisions in the shaping of scientific progress are made by individual investigators when they embark on a particular line of inquiry. The independent investigator is to-day usually a professional scientist, appointed by the public authorities on the basis of his scientific record to a post where he is expected to do research. He is given freedom to use his own time for research and is given control over means in money and personnel.

The granting of such discretion to individuals for the purposes of their profession is fairly common in all departments of life. Holders of higher posts in Business, Politics, the Law, Medicine, the Army, the Church, are all invested with powers which enable them to follow their own judgment within the framework of certain rules and to use this freedom in order to discharge their duties. Yet the degree of independence granted to the scientist may appear to be greater than that allowed to other professional men. A business man's duty is to make profits, a judge's to find the law, a general's to defeat the enemy; while in each case the choice of the specific means for fulfilling their task is left to the judgment of the person in charge, the standards of success are laid down for them from outside. For the scientist this does not hold to the same extent. It is part of his commission to revise and renew by pioneer achievements the very standards by which his work is to be judged. He may be denied full recognition for a considerable time—and yet his claims may be ultimately vindicated. But the difference is only one of degree. All standards of professional success undergo some change in the course of professional practice, and on the other hand even the most daring pioneer in science accepts the general conceptions of scientific achievement and bases his scientific claims essentially on traditional standards.

In any case, the powers to use his own intuitive judgment and the encouragement to embark on original lines of inquiry are not given to the scientist to enable him to pursue his own personal wishes. The high degree of independence he enjoys is granted only to enable him to discharge the more effectively his professional obligations. His task is to discover the opportunities in the given state of science for the most successful application of his own talents and to devote himself to the exploitation of these openings. The wider his freedom, the more fully can he throw the force of his personal conviction into the attack on his own problem.

At the start his task is yet hidden, but it is none the less definite. There is ample evidence to show that at any moment the next possibilities of discovery in science are few. The next step to be taken in any particular field is in fact sometimes so clear that we read of a "dramatic race" between leading scientists for an impending discovery. A series of such races took place within a period of a few years for the discovery of the synthesis of various vitamins. In 1935 Karrer in Zürich and Kuhn in Heidelberg competed in the synthesis of Vitamin B_2. In 1936 three teams, Andersag and Westphal in Germany, Williams and Cline in the United States and Todd and Bergel in England raced for the synthesis of Vitamin B_1. And in 1938 one of the participants in the B_1 race, Todd, and one in the B_2 race, Karrer, rivalled closely in the synthesis of Vitamin E. Only a few years earlier (1930) a great race was won in physics when Cockcroft and Walton, working under Rutherford's guidance in Cambridge, accomplished the artificial disintegration of the atom by electric discharge—ahead of Lange and Brasch in Germany and Breit, Tuve, Hafstad, Lauritsen, Lawrence and others in America. Or to take an example in pure theoretical physics: between 1920 and 1925 the standing problem of theoretical physicists was the reconciliation of classical mechanics and quantum theory; and around the year 1925, a number of physicists (de Broglie, Heisenberg, Born, Schrödinger, Dirac) did actually discover—more or less independently—the various parts of the solution. In a review of Eve's biography of Rutherford, Sir Charles Darwin[2] roughly estimates by how much Rutherford may have anticipated his contemporaries with his various discoveries and suggests for most cases spans of time ranging from a few months to three or four years. Rutherford himself is quoted as saying that no one can see more than an eighth of an inch beyond his nose and that only a great man can look even as far as that.

Scientific research is not made less creative nor less independent by the fact that at any particular time only a few discoveries are possible. We do not think less of the genius of Columbus because there was only one New World on this planet for him to discover.

2. *Nature,* 3670, Vol. 145, p. 324, 2nd March, 1940.

Though the task is definite enough, the finding of the solution is none the less intuitive. It is essential to start in science with the right guess about the direction of further progress. The whole career of a scientist often remains linked to the development of the single subject which stimulated his earliest guesses. All along the scientist is constantly collecting, developing and revising a set of half-conscious surmises, an assortment of private clues, which are his confidential guides to the mastery of his subject.

This loose system of intuitions cannot be formulated in definite terms. It represents a personal outlook which can be transmitted only—and very imperfectly at that—to personal collaborators who can watch for a year or two its daily application to the current problems of the laboratory. This outlook is as much emotional as it is intellectual. The expectations which it entertains are no idle guesses, but active hopes filled with enthusiasm.

The emotions of the scientist also express and uphold the values guiding research; they turn with admiration to courage and reliability and pour scorn on the commonplace and the fanciful. Such emotions again can be transmitted only by direct contact in the course of active collaboration. The leader of a research school has no more important function than to maintain enthusiasm for research among his students and instil in them the love of his own particular field.

Such is the calling of the scientist. The state of knowledge and the existing standards of science define the range within which he must find his task. He has to guess in which field and to what new problem his own special gifts can be most fruitfully applied. At this stage his gifts are still undisclosed, the problem is yet obscure. There is in him a hidden key, capable of opening a hidden lock. There is only one force which can reveal both key and lock and bring the two together: the creative urge which is inherent in the faculties of man and which guides them instinctively to the opportunities for their manifestation. The world outside can help by teaching, encouragement and criticism, but all the essential decisions leading to discovery remain personal and intuitive. No one with the least experience of a higher art or of any function requiring higher judgment, could conceive it to be possible that decisions such as these could be taken by one person for another. Decisions of this kind can in fact only be suppressed by the attempt to transfer them to an outside authority.

II

The scientist to-day cannot practise his calling in isolation. He must occupy a definite position within a framework of institutions. A chemist becomes a member of the chemical profession; a zoologist, a mathematician or a psychologist— each belongs to a particular group of specialized scientist. The different groups of scientists together form the *scientific community*.

The opinion of this community exercises a profound influence on the course of every individual investigation. Broadly speaking, while the choice of subjects and the actual conduct of research is entirely the responsibility of the individual scientist, the recognition of claims to discoveries is under the jurisdiction of scientific opinion expressed by scientists as a body. Scientific opinion exercises its power largely informally, but partly also by the use of an organized machinery. At any particular time only a certain range of subjects is deemed by this opinion to be profitable for scientific work and, accordingly, no training or posts are offered outside these fields, either for teaching or for research, while existing research schools and journals available for publication will also be restricted to these subjects.

In fact, even within the fields recognized at any particular time, scientific papers can be published only with the preliminary approval of two or three independent referees, called in as advisers by the editor of the journal. The referees express an opinion particularly on two points: whether the claims of the paper are sufficiently well substantiated and whether it possesses a sufficient degree of scientific interest to be worth publishing. Both characteristics are assessed by conventional standards which change with the passage of time according to the variations of scientific opinion. Sometimes it may be felt that the tendency among authors is towards too much speculation, which the referees will then try to correct by imposing more discipline. At other times there may seem to be a danger of absorption in mere mechanical work, which referees will again try to curb by insisting that papers should show more penetration and originality. Naturally at different periods there are also marked variations as regards the conclusions that are considered sufficiently plausible. A few years ago there was a period in which it was easy to get a paper printed claiming the transformation of chemical elements by ordinary laboratory processes[3]; to-day—as in earlier times—this would be found difficult, if not altogether impossible.

The referees advising scientific journals will also encourage to some extent those lines of research which they consider to be particularly promising, whilst discouraging other lines of which they have a poor opinion. The dominant powers in this respect, however, are exercised by referees advising on scientific appointments, on the allocation of special subsidies and on the award of distinctions. Advice on

3. Comp. my *Science, Faith and Society* (1946), p. 76.

these points, which often involve major issues of the policy of science, is usually asked from and tendered by a small number of senior scientists who are universally recognized as the most eminent in a particular branch. They are the chief Influentials, the unofficial governors of the scientific community. By their advice they can either delay or accelerate the growth of a new line of research. They can provide special subsidies for new lines of research at any moment. By the award of prizes and of other distinctions, they can invest a promising pioneer almost overnight with a position of authority and independence. More slowly, but no less effectively, a new development can be stimulated by the policy pursued by the Influentials in advising on new appointments. Within a decade or so a new school of thought can be established by the selection of appropriate candidates for Chairs which have fallen vacant during that period. The same end can be advanced even more effectively by the setting up of new Chairs.

The constant re-direction of scientific interest by the leaders of scientific opinion, fulfils the important function of keeping the standards of performance in the different branches of science approximately at an equal level. This level is jointly characterized by three factors: (1) the intrinsic interest of the subject-matter, which may be contemplative or practical. (2) the profundity or systematic interest of the generalizations involved and (3) the certainty and precision of the new statements made. In every branch of science this threefold valuation will have to be applied jointly, due regard being given particularly to the wide variations in the intrinsic interest of different subject-matters. Accordingly, less precision and systematic coherence will be required for example in the study of living matter and of human beings in particular, than in the study of inanimate bodies. The leaders of scientific opinion are responsible for maintaining all along the advancing frontier of science approximately uniform standards of value. Guided by these standards, they will keep shifting resources and encouragement to the more successful growing points of science, at the expense of the less fruitful sections; which will produce a tendency towards the most economical utilization of the total resources available to science, both in brainpower and in money.

The steady equalization of standards in all branches is necessary, not only in order to maintain a rational distribution of resources and recruits for research schools throughout the field of science, but also in order to uphold in every branch the authority of science with regard to the general public. With the relation of science and the public I shall presently deal in some detail. But a particular aspect of it requires mention at this stage, since it involves the final phase of the process by which recognition is given to new scientific claims. Published papers are open to discussion and their results may remain controversial for a while. But scientific controversies are usually settled—or else shelved to await further evidence—within a reasonable time. The results then pass over into textbooks for universities and schools and become part of generally accepted opinion. This final process of codification is again under the control of the body of scientific opinion, as expressed by reviews, under whose authority textbooks are brought into circulation.

The standards of science—like those of all other arts and professions—are transmitted largely by tradition. Science in the modern sense originated some 300 years ago from the work of a small number of pioneers, among whom Vesalius and Galileo, Boyle, Harvey and Newton were pre-eminent. The founders of modern science have discussed extensively and with considerable insight the new methods which they applied; moreover, the doctrines of the contemporary philosophy—particularly through John Locke—gave full expression to their outlook. Yet the core of the scientific method lies in the practical example of its works. Whatever the various philosophies of the scientific method may still reveal, modern science must continue to be defined as the search for truth on the lines set by the examples of Galileo and his contemporaries. No pioneer of science, however revolutionary—neither Pasteur, Darwin, Freud nor Einstein —has denied the validity of that tradition, nor even relaxed it in the least.

Modern science is a local tradition and is not easily transmitted from one place to another. Countries such as Australia, New Zealand, South Africa, Argentina, Brazil, Egypt, Mexico, have built great modern cities with spacious universities, but they have rarely succeeded in founding important schools of research. The current scientific production of these countries before the war was still less than the single contributions of either Denmark, Sweden or Holland. Those who have visited parts of the world where scientific life is just beginning, know of the back-breaking struggle that the lack of scientific tradition imposes on the pioneers. Here research work stagnates for lack of stimulus, there it runs wild in the absence of any proper directive influence. Unsound reputations grow like mushrooms: based on nothing but commonplace achievements, or even on mere empty boasts. Politics and business play havoc with appointments and the granting of subsidies for research. However rich the fund of local genius may be, such environment will fail to bring it to fruition. In the early phase in question, New Zealand loses its Rutherford, Australia its Alexander and its Bragg, and such losses retard further the growth of science in a new country. Rarely, if ever, was the final acclimatization of science outside Europe achieved, until the government of a country succeeded in inducing a few scientists from some traditional centre to settle down in their territory and to develop there a new home for scientific life, moulded on their own traditional standards. This demonstrates perhaps most vividly the fact that science as a whole is based—in the same way as the practice of any single research school—on a local tradition, consisting of a fund of intuitive approaches and emotional values, which can be transmitted from one generation to the other only through the medium of personal collaboration.

Scientific research—in short—is an art; it is the art of making certain kinds of discoveries. The scientific profession as a whole has the function of cultivating that art by transmitting and developing the tradition of its practise. The value which we attribute to science—whether its progress be considered good, bad or indifferent from a chosen point of view—does not matter here. Whatever that value may be, it still remains true that the tradition of science as an art can be handed on only by those practising that art. There can be therefore no question of another authority replacing scientific opinion for the purposes of this function; and any attempt to do so can result only in a clumsy distortion and—if persistently applied—in the more or less complete destruction of the tradition of science.

III

Professional scientists form a very small minority in the community, perhaps one in ten thousand. The ideas and opinions of so small a group can be of importance only by virtue of the response which they evoke from the general public. This response is indispensable to science, which depends on it for money to pay the costs of research and for recruits to replenish the ranks of the profession. Clearly, science can continue to exist on the modern scale only so long as the authority it claims is accepted by large groups of the public.

Why do people decide to accept science as valid? Can they not see the limitations of scientific demonstrations—in the pre-selected evidence, the pre-conceived theories, the always basically deficient documentation? They may see these shortcomings, or at least they may be made to see them. The fact remains that they must make up their minds about their material surroundings in one way or another. Men must form ideas about the material universe and must embrace definite convictions on the subject. No part of the human race has ever been known to exist without a system of such convictions and it is clear that their absence would mean intellectual annihilation. The public must choose, therefore, either to believe in science or else in some rival explanation of nature, such as that offered by Aristotle, the Bible, Astrology or Magic. Of all such alternatives the public of our times has in its majority chosen science.

This acceptance of science was achieved gradually through centuries of struggles which I will not try to recount here. But the victory was not complete and it is not necessarily final. Pockets of anti-scientific views persist in various forms. For instance, scientific medicine is rejected by that part of the public in Western countries which professes Christian Science; fundamentalism challenges geology and evolution; astrology has a more or less vague ascendancy in wide circles; spiritualism carries on a borderline existence between science and mysticism. These persistent centres of heterodoxy are a constant challenge to science. It is not inconceivable that from one of these there may emerge in the future some element of truth inaccessible to the scientific method, which might form the starting-point of a new interpretation of nature. In any case, these anti-scientific movements constitute at present an effective test of the spontaneous acceptance of science: their failure to spread their doctrines further shows that science remains considerably more convincing than any other of the possible alternatives.

IV

I have shown that the forces contributing to the growth and dissemination of science operate in three stages. The individual scientists take the initiative in choosing their problems and conducting their investigations; the body of scientists controls each of its members by imposing the standards of science; and finally the people decide in public discussion whether or not to accept science as the true explanation of nature. At each stage a human will operates. But this exercise of will is fully determined on each occasion by the responsibility inherent in the action; hence any attempt to direct these actions from outside must inevitably distort or destroy their proper meaning.

There are two recent instances on record of attempts made to break the autonomy of scientific life and to subordinate it to State direction. The one made by National Socialist Germany was so crude and cynical that it is easy to demonstrate its purely destructive nature. Take the following utterances attributed to Himmler, in which he reproved German scholars who refused to accept as genuine a forged document concerning German pre-history:

> We don't care a hoot whether this or something else was the real truth about the pre-history of the German tribes. Science proceeds from hypotheses that change every year or two. So there's no earthly reason why the party should not lay down a particular hypothesis as the starting-point, even if it runs counter to current scientific opinion. The one and only thing that matters to

us, and the thing these people are paid for by the State, is to have ideas of history that strengthen our people in their necessary national pride.[4]

Clearly, Himmler only pretended here—as a mere form of words—that he wished to readjust the foundations of science; his actual purpose was to suppress free inquiry in order to consolidate a particular falsehood which he considered useful. The philosophical difficulties in the position of science were used only in order to confuse the issue and to cloak—however thinly—an act of sheer violence.

V

The attempts of the Soviet Government to start a new kind of science are on an altogether different level. They represent a genuine effort to run science for the public good and they provide therefore a proper test of the principles involved in such an attempt.

I shall illustrate the process and its results by the example of genetics and plant-breeding, to which governmental direction was applied with particular energy.[5] The intervention of the State in these fields began about the year 1930 and was definitely established by the All-Union Conference on the Planning of Genetics and Selection held in Leningrad in 1932. Up to that time genetics developed and greatly flourished in Russia as a free science, guided by the

4. H. Rauschning, *Hitler Speaks* (1939), pp. 224–5.

5. Note that the date of writing is December 1942. I have left the account unchanged for its historical interest in showing the position of the Genetics Controversy, as it appeared at the time. This, I believe, was the first paper to draw attention to the danger involved in it to science in general.

standards that were recognized throughout the world. The Conference of 1932 decided that genetics and plant-breeding should henceforth be conducted with a view to obtaining immediate practical results and on lines conforming to the official doctrine of dialectical materialism, research being directed by the State.[6]

No sooner had these blows been delivered against the autonomy of science than the inevitable consequences set in. Any person claiming a discovery in genetics and plant-breeding could henceforth appeal directly over the heads of scientists to gullible practitioners or to political officials. Spurious observations and fallacious theories advanced by dilettants, cranks and impostors could thus gain currency, unchecked by scientific criticism.

An important case of this kind was that of I. V. Michurin, (1855–1935) a plant-breeding farmer, who some years earlier had announced the discovery of new strains of plants produced by grafting. He claimed to have achieved revolutionary improvements in agriculture, and to have obtained a striking confirmation of dialectical materialism. The opinion of science, on the contrary, was—and still remains—that Michurin's observations were mere illusions and referred to a spurious phenomenon, known by the name of "vegetative hybridization" which had been frequently described before. The illusion can arise from an incomplete statistical analysis of the results obtained, and may be occasionally supported

6. The Communist Academy, founded in 1926, which had originally been entrusted with the direction of science in the light of dialectical materialism, gained no ascendancy over the research work of non-party scientists. The inauguration of the policy described in the text coincided with the dissolution of the Scientific Section of the Communist Academy and represented a replacement of its functions by a more general, if much less extreme, application of the principles of dialectical materialism.

also by the fact that viruses are transmitted to the graft and its offsprings. The occurrence of true hereditary hybridization by grafting would be incompatible with the very foundations of modern biological science and its existence had been decisively discredited by the formulation of Mendel's laws and the discoveries of cytogenetics.

The new policy of the Soviet Government, inaugurated in 1932, paralysed the force of scientific opinion, which had barred the way to the acceptance of Michurin's claims. His work appealed to the practical agronomist and it conformed to the official philosophy of the State. It thus fulfilled both the practical and political criteria which had replaced the standards of science. Hence—quite logically —Michurin's work was given official recognition. The Government, in its enthusiasm over this first fruit of its new policy in science, went even further and erected a monument to Michurin, by re-naming the town of Koslov and calling it "Michurinsk" in his honour (1932).

The breach thus made in the autonomy of science laid the field of genetics and plant-breeding wide open to further invasion by spurious claims. The leader of this invasion became T. D. Lysenko—a successful worker in agricultural technique—who expanded Michurin's claims into a new theory of heredity which he set up in opposition to Mendelism and cytogenetics. His popular influence caused hundreds of people without proper scientific training, such as farmers and young students of agriculture, to attempt grafting experiments with the aim of producing "vegetative hybrids." Lysenko has himself described proudly how by the labours of this mass movement vegetative hybrids "poured out like the fruits from the horn of abundance."[7] Aided by

7. Lysenko's speech at the Conference on Genetics and Selection, Moscow 1939, quoted in the following as C.G.S. 1939.

claims of this kind, Lysenko gained high recognition by the government. He was appointed a member of the Academy of the U.S.S.R. and made President of the Academy of Agricultural Science of the U.S.S.R. By 1939 his influence had reached the point that he could induce the Commissariat of Agriculture to prohibit the methods hitherto used in plant-breeding stations and to introduce, compulsorily, new ones that were based on his own doctrine of heredity and that were contrary to accepted scientific opinion.[8] In a publication of the same year he even went so far as to demand the final elimination of his scientific opponents, by the total abolition of genetics in Russia: "In my opinion" —he wrote—"it is quite time to remove Mendelism entirely from university courses and from the theoretical and practical guidance of seed-raising."[9]

However, the Government hesitated to take this decisive step and a conference was called to clarify the situation. The Editors of the Journal *Under the Banner of Marxism* acted as conveners, and the proceedings, together with an extensive editorial commentary, were subsequently published in that Journal.[10] The reports of this Conference form impressive evidence of the rapid and radical destruction of a branch of science, caused clearly by the fact that the conduct of research had been placed under the direction of the State. We may note that the government in this case was a particularly progressive one and that it was aiming at solid benefits for

8. Vavilov's speech, C.G.S. 1939.

9. Quoted by N. P. Doubinin in his speech at the C.G.S. 1939, from Lysenko, *The Mentor an all-powerful tool in selection,* p. 38, 1939.

10. Translated extracts from the Conference Report were made available to me by courtesy of the Society for Cultural Relations with the U.S.S.R. The translation was checked and revised by reference to the original test.

its own people. It is all the more significant that in spite of this, the result of its action was only to plunge the science of genetics into a morass of corruption and confusion.

The Conference which revealed these conditions to the outside observer was presided over by M. B. Mitin (a person unknown to international science and probably a representative of the Journal), who in his opening speech outlined once again the practical and theoretical principles to which science had to conform under the direction of the Soviet State. "We have no gulf between theory and practice, we have no Chinese wall between scientific achievements and practical activity. Every genuine discovery, every genuine scientific achievement is with us translated into practice, enters into the life of hundreds of institutions, attracts the attention of the mass of people by its fruitful results. Soviet biologists, geneticists and selectionists must understand dialectical and historical materialism, and learn to apply the dialectical method to their scientific work. Verbal, formal acceptance of dialectical materialism is not wanted."

Academician N. I. Vavilov, internationally recognized as the most eminent geneticist in Russia (as shown by his election as Foreign Member of the Royal Society) put the case for the science of genetics. He surveyed the development of this science from its inception and pointed out that not a single author of repute anywhere outside Russia would either doubt the soundness of cytogenetics, or would be prepared to accept the existence of so-called "vegetative hybrids."

Such appeals however had by now lost their substance; with the establishment of State supremacy over science, the authority of international scientific opinion had been rendered void. Vavilov was rightly answered by confronting him with his own declaration, made at the Planning Conference of 1932, in which he had deprecated the cultivation of science for its own purpose. Yielding at the time perhaps to pressure, or believing it wise to meet popular tendencies half-way and little expecting the far-reaching consequences which were to follow from the abandonment of his true principles—he had given way to the point of saying: "The divorce of genetics from practical selection, which characterizes the research work of the U.S.A., England and other countries, must be resolutely removed from genetics-selection research in the U.S.S.R."[11]

Now that such principles were generally accepted, Vavilov could raise no legitimate objection if the classical experiments to which he referred, and on which his branch of science was based, were laughed to scorn by men like the practical plant-breeder V. K. Morozov—who addressed the meeting as follows: "The representatives of formal genetics say that they get good 3:1 ratio results with *Drosophila*. Their work with this object is very profitable to them, because the affair, as one might say, is irresponsible . . . if the flies die, they are not penalized." In Morozov's opinion a science which in twenty years had produced no important practical results at his plant-breeding station, could not possibly be sound.[12]

This view may in fact be considered as a correct conclusion from the criteria of science now officially accepted (though fortunately by no means universally enforced) in the Soviet Union. If all the evidence drawn from cases not important in practice is to be disregarded or at least treated lightly, then little proof can remain in support of the theories of genetics. Under such circumstances any simple,

11. Proceedings of the All-Union Conference on planning Genetics-Selection research, Leningrad, June 29th, 1932, p. 21. Academy of Science of U.S.S.R., Leningrad 1933, quoted by Lysenko in his speech at C.G.S. 1939.

12. Morozov's speech, C.G.S. 1939.

plausible idea such as the fallacies advocated by Lysenko must inevitably acquire greater convincing power and gain wider support among all non-specialists, whether practitioners or ordinary laymen. This is in fact what the Conference on Genetics demonstrated. Morozov could assure Lysenko that nearly all practical field workers, agronomists and collective farmers had become followers of his doctrine of heredity.

The authority of science having been replaced by that of the State, it was only logical that political arguments should be used against Vavilov's traditional scientific reasoning. Lysenko for example said: "N. I. Vavilov knows that one cannot defend Mendelism before Soviet readers by writing down its foundation, by recounting what it consists of. It has become particularly impossible nowadays when millions of people possess such a mighty theoretical weapon as *The Short Course of the History of the All-Union Communist Party (Bolshevists)*. When he grasps Bolshevism, the reader will not be able to give his sympathy to metaphysics, and Mendelism definitely is pure, undisguised metaphysics."[13] It was logical again that Lysenko and his adherents should invoke Michurin as an authority whose claims had been established by the State; that Lysenko should speak of "that genius of biology I. V. Michurin, recognized by the Party and the Government and by the country . . ." and declare that it is "false and conceited" on the part of a biologist to think that he could add anything to Michurin's teachings.

Indeed, in such circumstances there seems nothing left to the hard-pressed scientists but to attempt a defence in the same terms as used by their opponents. This is what

13. This passage is quoted by Lysenko in his speech at the C.G.S. 1939 from an article published by himself in *Socialist Agriculture,* Feb. 1939. In his speech Lysenko reaffirms this statement.

the eminent geneticist Professor N. P. Doubinin apparently decided to do at the Conference on Genetics. His speech in defence of cytogenetics refers freely to Marx, Engels and the *Short Course of the History of the Communist Party*. He reverently mentions Michurin, naming him as a classic next to Darwin. But in his view—as he explains—all these high authorities are directly or indirectly supporting Mendelism. "It is quite wrong," he says, "to describe Mendelism by saying that its appearance represents a product of the imperialist development of capitalist society. Of course, after its appearance Mendelism was perverted by bourgeois scientists. We know well the fact that all science is class science."

Such is the last stage in the collapse of science. Attackers and defenders are using the same spurious and often fanciful arguments, to enlist for their own side the support of untutored practitioners and of equally untutored politicians. But the position of the defenders is hopeless. Science cannot be saved on grounds which contradict its own basic principles. The ambitious and unscrupulous figures who rise to power on the tide of a movement against science, do not withdraw when scientists make their last abject surrender. On the contrary, they stay to complete their triumph by directing against their yielding opponents the charge of insincerity. Thus Lysenko says, "The Mendelian geneticists keep silent about their own radical disagreement with the theory of development, with the teaching of Michurin," and even more jeering is the taunt made by Lysenko's assistant Professor I. I. Prezent: "It is new to find that all of them, some more sincerely than others, all of them try to give the impression that with Michurin at least they have no quarrel."[14]

14. Quoted by Kolbanovsky in his summary of the C.G.S., 1939.

Such taunts are unanswerable and their implications are shattering. They make it clear that scientists must never hope to save their scientific pursuits by creeping under the cloak of anti-scientific principles. "Verbal, formal acceptance of these principles"—the Chairman had sternly warned from the beginning—"is not wanted."[15]

VI

The demonstration given here of the corruption of a branch of science, caused by placing its pursuit under the direction of the State, seems to me complete. Particularly, as there can be no doubt of the unwavering desire of the Soviet Government to advance the progress of science. It has spent large sums on laboratories, on equipment and on personnel. Yet these subsidies, we have seen, benefited science only so long as they flowed into channels controlled by independent scientific opinion, whereas as soon as their allocation was accompanied by attempts at establishing governmental direction, they exercised a destructive influence.

We may hope and expect that one day the Soviet Government will recognize the error of such attempts; that they will realize, for example, that their plant-breeding stations are operating on lines which were abandoned as fallacious in the rest of the world about forty years earlier.

15. Note added in December 1949: The Conference on Genetics and Selection held in 1939 was followed within a year by the dismissal of Vavilov from the directorship of the Institute of Plant Industry. He was subsequently imprisoned and died, without any announcement or explanation, probably in 1943. (Eric Ashby, *Scientist in Russia,* p. 111). The Conference which I have analysed at some length here appears to have been the last occasion on which Vavilov publicly defended the scientific theory of heredity.

What can a government do when it realizes such a state of affairs? What course can it then take to restore the functions of science?

According to our analysis the answer cannot be in doubt. One thing only is necessary—but that is truly indispensable. All that is required is to restore the independence of scientific opinion—to restore fully its powers of maintaining scientific standards, through the selection of papers for publication, through the selection of candidates for scientific posts, through the granting of scientific distinctions and in the award of special research subsidies; to restore to scientific opinion the power of controlling by its influence the publication of textbooks and popularizations of science, and the teaching of science in universities and schools; to restore to it above all the power of protecting that most precious foothold of originality, the position of the independent scientist—who must again become sole master of his own research work.

There would still be time to revive the great scientific tradition of Russia which, although at present distorted in many respects, is far from being dead. The recent great progress of Russian mathematics, and of many other fields in which State control has never been effectively applied, proves that the valuation of science for its own sake still lives in the U.S.S.R. Let scientists be free once more to expound their true ideals and be allowed to appeal to the Soviet peoples, asking for their support of science on its own grounds. Let them be free to expose the cranks and careerists who have infiltrated into their ranks since the inception of "planning"' in 1932 and let them become affiliated once more to the body of international science.

The very moment that scientists regain these freedoms, science will flourish again and will rise overnight, free of all the confusion and corruption which is now affecting it.

VII

However, the current of future events may well tend towards the very opposite course. Even in countries where science is still free we are experiencing to-day a weakening of the principles of scientific autonomy. "Science must be marshalled for the people"—Professor H. Levy proclaimed amidst applause at a popular rally of scientists in London.[16] Fired by misguided generosity, these scientists would sacrifice science—forgetting that it is theirs only on trust for the purpose of cultivation, not theirs to give away and allow to perish.

Our analysis seems to leave no doubt that if this kind of movement prevailed and developed further: if attempts to suppress the autonomy of science, such as have been made in Russia since 1932, became world-wide and were persisted in for a time, the result could only be a total destruction of science and of scientific life.

16. Conference of the Association of Scientific Workers on "The Planning of Science," January, 1943.

5

Science and Welfare[1]

I

The popular scientific books which I used to read as a child were mainly concerned with displaying the wonders of nature and the glorious achievements of science. They dwelt on the enormous distances between the stars and on the laws governing their motion; on the crowd of living creatures made visible in a drop of water under the microscope. Among the best-sellers of the time was Darwin's *Origin of Species* and every new discovery throwing light on the process of evolution roused a wide, popular curiosity. Such were the topics and interests that came first to the mind in connection with science at that time. It was not forgotten of course that science provided also a store of most useful knowledge; but this was not considered as its principal justification. New practical inventions like the electromotor or the wireless telegraph were regarded as merely occasional off-shoots of advancing scientific knowledge.

To-day boys and girls who are interested in science are given a very different interpretation of it. They read books

1. Expanded from *The Political Quarterly* (1945).

which profess that the primary function of science is to promote human welfare. The best-seller in the field has been for the last seven years Hogben's *Science for the Citizen,* which was closely rivalled in its success by J. G. Crowther's books, particularly the *Social Relations of Science* and the famous *Social Functions of Science* by J. D. Bernal.[2] These books emphatically oppose the view, generally accepted before, that science should be pursued for the sake of enlightenment, regardless of its practical use. They have exercised a powerful popular influence which has been consolidated lately by the support of important organizations. It has in fact become rare to find any public statement to-day which would declare it clearly that the main purpose of science is the acquisition of knowledge for its own sake. Such a conception of science is still generally maintained by the academic profession; but it is no exaggeration to say that the broader public is beginning to forget it, even though it had universally accepted it only fifteen years ago.

The new radically utilitarian valuation of science rests on a consistent philosophical background, borrowed mainly from Marxism. It denies that pure science, as distinct from applied or technical science, can exist at all. Such a revaluation of science necessarily leads to a demand for the Planning of Science. If science is to serve the practical needs of society it must be properly organized for this purpose. You cannot expect individual scientists, each pursuing his particular interests, to develop science effectively towards the satisfaction of existing social needs. You must see to it therefore that scientists are placed under the guidance of authorities who know the needs of society and are generally responsible for safe-guarding the public interest. We are as-

2. For a detailed critique of Bernal's book see my *The Contempt of Freedom* (1940), the essay entitled "The Rights and Duties of Science."

sured by its advocates that this form of organization is not only logical but quite practicable, since in Soviet Russia it has already been successfully applied. It is urged that we have only to follow (in our own way) the Russian example.

The plea for the planning of science is reinforced further by a materialistic interpretation of the history of science. In its light the supposed independence of scientific progress appears as a mere illusion. Science, it would seem, has actually always advanced only in response to social needs. The representatives of this theory have given elaborate analyses of the history of science, purporting to show how each step forward was socially determined. Thus the planning of science, they urge, would merely bring into the open the existing position of science and there could be no question of any violence done thereby to its spirit. The protest of those who would defend the freedom of science against planning is rejected and branded as an expression of an obsolete and socially irresponsible attitude.

II

I shall now examine in the light of the relevant facts the principal proposition which underlies the movement for the planning of science. Let us see whether there *is* or *is not* any essential difference between pure and applied science; such a difference as would justify and demand the separate pursuit of the two branches of knowledge, by different methods and under distinctive conditions. We shall take one characteristic field of pure science and one of applied science, and compare the two.

As an example of *pure science* we take the science of mechanics, the great model of all sciences through the ages. The story begins with Copernicus. On his deathbed 400 years ago, he gave to the world the first published copy of his long delayed work *De Revolutionibus*. The regular motions of the planets had been observed and mapped out for thousands of years before, as a pattern of wheels within wheels, of cycles and epicycles. Copernicus showed that most of these complications were due to the awkward position from which the heavenly events were observed. He now pictured the sun centrally with the six hitherto known planets surrounding it in circular orbits. This simpler picture was of striking beauty and carried great powers of conviction.

Copernicus, the Pole, was followed by the German Kepler, who took his stand on the Copernican system, but broke the spell of the cycles and epicycles which had survived in it. Kepler denied these ancient harmonies and established in their place three laws which still bear his name. The planets, he said, move along elliptic orbits, having the sun in one of their foci, in such a fashion that the line drawn from the planet to the sun sweeps out equal areas in equal times and the squares of the periods of planetary revolutions are proportional to the cubes of the planetary distances. These laws foreshadowed the work of Newton. But before Newton could set to work, yet another giant step had to be accomplished by the Florentine, Galileo. He made experiments on falling bodies and found that objects of different weight fall at the same rate. He was the first to formulate such results in mathematical terms. Galileo and Kepler mutually encouraged each other by correspondence; but they did not remotely surmise that the laws which each had discovered in his own field, one on earth and the other in the skies, were really identical. They were both dead long before this was discovered by Newton.

An entire century had passed since the death of Copernicus before Newton was born and forty-five years of his life elapsed before he published the *Principia*, the book which first brought the whole universe under the rule of one mathematical law. From the falling of the stone on earth it predicted the revolutions of the moon and went on to derive all the laws which Kepler established for the planets. This discovery completed the intellectual progress started by Copernicus 150 years earlier. To the medieval view the universe had been a place just large enough to allow comfortable space for our Earth, with a dome of stars serving as a lid, or shell, at a suitable distance around it. This cosy shelter of man was now destroyed. He and his Earth were thrown out of the centre of things and relegated to an obscure peripheric position; the Earth, reduced to a mere roaming speck, plunged into an infinite emptiness. At the same time man's immediate surroundings were subordinated to the mathematical laws governing a universe of stars.

Thus Newton radically transformed the outlook of man and people felt that through him science had unravelled the mystery of the universe. High honours were given to him, and at his death he was buried in Westminster, with great peers of the realm as his pall-bearers. His college in Cambridge erected a statue with the inscription "Newton qui ingenio humanam gentem superavit" ("Newton who mentally surpassed the human race"). The writers of the French Enlightenment, including Voltaire himself, were prompted to produce popular presentations of Newton's theory for the Continental public. Far beyond the borders of science Newton's discovery determined the method in all departments of thought. Thinkers from Rousseau to Marx and Herbert Spencer dreamed of discovering some master formula governing human matters, as Newton's laws governed the material universe.

Meanwhile the rigorous scientific evaluation of Newton's laws progressed apace. For a hundred years after Newton's death the greatest mathematicians of the time were engaged in recasting Newton's laws. D'Alembert, Lagrange, Maupertuis, Laplace, Hamilton, each in his turn revealed further the depth and beauty of these laws and added to their powers to solve a variety of problems.

Yet, looking back to-day, all this seems only the beginning. Vast discoveries were to follow, destined to be born to our own century. One of their main starting-points was a comparatively slight observation on the light emitted by discharge tubes such as are used in neon signs. Its analysis showed a remarkably regular assortment of colours. Towards the end of the last century a set of most curious numerical laws governing the wavelength of these colours was discovered by the Swiss physicist, Ritz. So striking were these laws, and seemingly so full of hidden significance, that the German physicist, Runge, was heard to exclaim about Ritz: "May I but live to see the Newton who will follow this Kepler!" Runge's desire was fulfilled by the advent in his lifetime of Max Planck (1900) and Niels Bohr (1912). In their hands and those of their successors a new form of mechanics took shape which included atomic processes. Through this advance, the science of mechanics extended its control right into the internal machinery of the atom: predicting colour and cohesion, mechanical resistance and electrical conductivity, it penetrated to the very essence of distinctive chemical properties.

Nor was that all; for about the same time yet another great transformation of mechanics took its origin in Einstein's new conception of space and time. Formulated in these new terms the laws of mechanics are further unified. Newton's laws of gravitation and his laws of motion were merged in one conception, which had come to include also the laws of electric forces discovered in the middle of the foregoing century by Maxwell. A wealth of detailed conclusions has since been drawn from the new mechanics, which will go on moulding our outlook on the universe for generations yet to come, as Newton's discovery did before.

Let us now glance briefly at a counter-example in the field of engineering or *applied science*. Take a field like artificial lighting, in which the application of science has lately been particularly effective. Primitive lighting was based on candles, torches and oil-lamps. At the beginning of the last century paraffin-lamps were introduced—which Goethe described as of dazzling brightness. Then came coal-gas with burners of various types, culminating in the incandescent mantle, which spread its yellow light over the supper table of my childhood. Electricity started with the arc-lamp, burning in the open air between poles made of graphite; soon to be superseded by Edison's great invention, the enclosed incandescent lamp. A little later came—as an attempt to revert to the open air—the "Nernst-burner" of great, though brief and now forgotten fame. And just before the war we saw the rapid advance of discharge lamps, like the mercury and sodium lamp, particularly for street lighting. We may find these in future displacing the incandescent lamp in most of its uses. And—making a guess into the more remote future—we may surmise that some time a new form of lighting, illuminating perhaps the whole countryside, may become possible through the use of artificial radioactivity.

Such is in brief outline the history of a great branch of scientific engineering. Let us see whether we can distinguish any radical difference between this and the development of a branch of pure science, described before. In doing so, we must eliminate all individual preferences: giving as warm an admiration to the ingenuity of inventions (say of the gas-mantle) as we do to an outstanding discovery in science (say in mechanics). There must be no question of the comparative *values* of pure and applied science; only of the fact whether the two are or are not essentially different intellectual activities.

On this point the above analysis can hardly leave room for hesitation. While the scientific method plays a part in both, the purpose pursued and the results achieved in the two cases are easily distinguishable. The intellectual events which start with Copernicus and end with Einstein form a process of continued penetration into the nature of things. It forms a series of discoveries into the laws of nature, ever widening in scope and delving ever further into greater depths. The history of lighting, on the other hand, teaches us little or nothing about the laws of nature. Occasionally the invention of new sources of light has led to very interesting observations. The development of gas lighting has taught us some new facts about the formation of coal-gas, and the lamp industry has contributed to our knowledge of tungsten at high temperatures. But these minor discoveries were clearly incidental to the main purpose of the lighting industry, which continued to be the production of ever cheaper and more convenient sources of light. Illumination as a branch of engineering would have been none the less successful had it led to no discoveries whatever on the nature of things.

Turning to pure science, on the other hand, we find exactly the opposite conditions. The development of astronomy and mechanics from Copernicus to Einstein has admittedly resulted in innumerable practical advances; in fact there is no end to the occasions on which a knowledge of mechanics, both terrestrial and celestial, has proved useful to various crafts. But in this case the practical results were merely incidental to the overriding purpose of advancing knowledge. The science of mechanics would still be what it is, even though it had borne no practical fruits, and would count no less as a chapter of science.

The distinction between technology and pure science can be sharply defined by economic criteria. Applied science teaches how to produce practical advantages by the use of material resources. But there is a limit to the urgency of any particular practical advantage and a limit to the abundance of any particular resources. No technology can remain valid in the face of a sharp drop in the demand for its produce or a steep fall in the supply of its raw materials. Once it turns out goods that are of less value than the materials used up, the process becomes technically nonsensical. An invention designed to produce practical *disadvantages* cannot be regarded as an invention, either in the light of common sense or in the eyes of patent law. Pure science, on the other hand, cannot be affected in its validity by variations of supply or demand. The interest of one branch or another may thereby be altered slightly, but no particle of science will be invalidated: nothing will become nonsensical that was true before—nor the reverse.

This contrast between pure and applied science involves a profound difference in the logical structure of the two fields. The progress of mechanics, of which I have given an outline, through four centuries can be seen to go on continuing on the lines of the same basic ideas. Each new phase restates that which was known before and reveals that its predecessor was the embryo of a truth wider and deeper than itself. We are faced with a persistent unfolding of thought by logical stages. Technology progresses differently. Lighting is constantly made cheaper and pleasanter. To that extent the development is also consistent and continuous. But logically each forward step represents a new departure. There are no principles, unless the most trivial ones, which are common to the candle, the gas-burner and the incandescent lamp. Even between the four forms of electric lighting there is hardly a connecting thread of thought. Each new improved form of illumination simply displaces its predecessor. Instead of the development of a single principle, we see a series of logically disconnected attempts to serve a steady purpose.

This contrast in the logical structure of pure and applied science determines the difference in the proper conditions for the cultivation of each. Scientific work can progress logically only if guided by systematic principles. Here is the reason for the academic seclusion of science. A system of thought can be advanced only in the midst of a community which is thoroughly imbued with its understanding, which is both responsive and critical, and passionately devoted to the subject. Academic seclusion fostering a scientific atmosphere represents therefore an indispensable framework for a single-minded application to systematic science. There is room, no doubt, for reform in the existing organization of science, but the academic conditions required for its cultivation, rooted in the systematic nature of science, must be preserved.

Turning now to technological research, we again find that the nature of the task clearly determines the proper conditions under which it has to be pursued. There are many classes of inventions and technical improvements, but in no case has the inventor to immerse himself entirely in one branch of scientific knowledge, while it is indispensable that he should remain intensely aware of a certain set of practical circumstances. An inventor who lacks a keen sense of practical profitability will produce inventions which work only on paper. That is why inventions do not thrive on academic soil. Admittedly, some branches of engineering which have a systematic structure can be cultivated at universities and engineering science, understood in that sense, rightly relies for its advancement on technical schools and other academic institutions. But a far greater part of applied science consists of more or less disjointed solutions to problems which can be properly sensed and appreciated only by those struggling daily in the dust and heat of practical life.

III

Thus we come back to the plain truth which had long been known, before the great modern enlightenment succeeded in obscuring it: namely, that there exists *pure science* and *applied science*, quite distinct in nature and in conditions of cultivation; the first finding its home on academic soil, the second in the factories and other quarters closely attached to practical life.

The Planning of Science is supposed to conduct the pursuit of pure science towards discoveries which will be useful when applied to practical problems. That is in general impossible. Pure science has its own inherent aims and could embrace different aims only by ceasing to be what it is. It would have to discontinue the pursuit known to-day by the word "science" and substitute for it some other activity, which would not be science.

What would the new kind of "science" be like? Is it at all possible to pursue the discovery of new facts in nature with a mind to their prospective use for the solution of definite practical problems? Yes, in certain cases. It is a common practice in modern industry to make systematic studies of various materials in order to manufacture from them particular pieces of equipment. New drugs against diseases or pests are tried out in a similar fashion. There are various other cases in medicine, agriculture, mining, metallurgy, etc., where scientific investigations of a fairly high order can be conducted with a view to a definite practical application. But all these fields represent only a tiny fraction of the actual progress currently made by science and a planned science limited to investigations of this kind would therefore be a mere vestige of what science represents to-day.

We can speak here from experience. Institutions are by no means lacking which have the task of pursuing scientific research of definite practical importance. There are the

Research Associations investigating problems relevant to the various industries, such as cotton, coal, steel, glass and others. There are the institutions for agricultural and military research and the industrial research laboratories of private firms. In Britain, as in most other industrial countries, about the same amount is spent on this kind of research as on academic research. Yet the contributions thus made to science are very small. I doubt whether as much as one per cent. of the material which is being added annually to the textbooks of physics and chemistry, mathematics, botany and zoology, has its origin from investigations which were pursued with a view to their interest to some industry or other practical concern. To plan science within such limits would be simply to kill science.

Convinced believers in planning who realize these facts sometimes try to uphold their principles by pointing at the existing control of science. They point out that state grants for universities are fixed by legislative decision, and that the distribution of grants between the different branches of science is effected in the universities in the light of public responsibility. But the former decision merely adjusts the level of all scientific activities; while the latter only guides the resources thus allocated towards the points at which science is showing the strongest signs of spontaneous growth.[3] Only the total extent of the scientific effort is affected here, while its direction is left to follow freely the tendencies inherent in science.

Alternatively, convinced planners of science may try to save their principles by limiting their proposals to a very general and slight preference for certain directions of scientific research, and they may even add the promise that this would involve no reduction in any research pursued on other than the preferred lines. As an answer to the first point, we note

3. Comp. p. 65 above.

94

that an extraneous direction of science is mischievous precisely to the extent to which it is effective. It is no excuse for doing a perverse action on a small scale that the consequent damage is correspondingly small; it is less harmful to cut off a finger than a whole arm, but this does not justify the act. And as regards the promise that planning would leave unplanned activities unaffected, this is altogether specious. The mental and material resources of society cannot be both directed into new channels and left to flow into the old ones. The virtual cessation in wartime of progress in pure science, through the necessary diversion of scientific resources to defence work, has demonstrated this clearly enough.

IV

But how about the argument of historical materialism, insisting that the development of science can be represented at every step as a response to social needs? Take the widespread theory that Newton's work on gravitation arose in response to the expanding maritime interests of Britain.[4] Its expounders make no attempt to discover the maritime interests which stimulated the Pole Copernicus in Heilsberg, or the German Kepler in Prague, or the Florentine Galileo to labour during a century before Newton in laying down the foundations for his work. Nor do they pay attention to the overwhelming response given to Newton in countries, such as Switzerland and Prussia, not in the least interested in maritime problems. Swayed by an overriding

4. Thus J. G. Crowther, *The Social Relations of Science* (1941), p. 391: "The *Principia* may be regarded, to a large extent, as a theoretical synthesis of the problems set in gravity, circular motion, planetary and lunar movement, and the shape and size of the earth by the demand for better navigation."

95

materialistic prejudice, they never attempt to apply even the most elementary rules of critical thought.

Nevertheless, the idea that the direction in which science progresses is distinctly affected by the prevailing material needs, has become widely accepted even among people far remote from the Marxist camp. I want to place here on record, therefore, a more detailed refutation of some prominent statements from which this mode of thought has taken its origin.

The argument consists mainly in spotlighting the various connections of science with society, the personal reasons for which scientific work is undertaken, the materials required for its pursuit, the effects—whether good or bad—which result from it, while the inherent logic for scientific progress is left in the dark. Thus J. G. Crowther in *The Social Relations of Science* extensively scrutinizes the incomes of people who do or do not take up science. We learn that often people are too poor to be concerned with science and that in other cases they are too rich to trouble about it. Plato, for example, was rich and despised science,[5] and ever since rich people tend to follow him.[6] Very often it is, on the contrary, great wealth that promotes scientific interest, just as the right sort of poverty may do it.[7]

5. *Ibid.*, pp. 66–67.

6. p. 125, Platonism the carrier of anti-scientific snobbery in Roman times; p. 279, it becomes the philosophy of the ruling bankers of the Renaissance; p. 578, it is the first sketch of the philosophy of modern Fascism.

7. p. 116, the Romans were too rich to advance science; p. 160, so were the Moslems; p. 592, the French people after 1918 were also too rich; p. 552, Russian Academy before the Soviet Revolution misguided by wealth. On the other hand (p. 208) great wealth was helpful to Roger Bacon's scientific work; and also (p. 358) to Guericke's: and (p. 369) to Boyle's, and—in general—the status of a gentleman of leisure was the economic condition for scientific excellence throughout the Middle Ages

Such considerations are misleading, unless taken in a sense in which they are obvious and irrelevant. Whether a person can and will become a scientist or not clearly depends to some extent on his income and private circumstances. But once he has become a scientist, his results do not depend on his personal circumstances. The principle of Conservation of Energy was discovered independently by a cranky South German doctor (J. R. Mayer), a reputable beer-brewer in Manchester (Joule) and a young Prussian scientist (H. von Helmholtz). The three living co-discoverers of quantum mechanics (an Austrian, a Prussian and an Englishman) make an equally ill-assorted triplet. The greatest advance in physics made in Russia during the past twenty-five years was the observation in 1928 of a new form of optical scattering by the Soviet physicist Landsberg. The same discovery was made a few weeks earlier by C. V. Raman, a native and inhabitant of British India, who, in view of his priority, received the Nobel prize for this piece of work. He had, however, to share some of the credit with the Viennese physicist—sometime an ardent Nazi—A. Smekal, who predicted the effect a few years earlier. It is difficult to find three people as different in personality and social setting as Landsberg, Raman and Smekal, yet their work in science is essentially identical.

Science is again submerged in extraneous matters when the practical interest of society is emphasized to the point at which it appears that science itself is guided by that interest. The obvious fact that, with the exception of very few cases, no one can tell at the time of a discovery what its future practical applications will be; and that these applications are

---

(p. 239) and in sixteenth and seventeenth century England (p. 384). On the other hand, medieval society was too poor for the advancement of science (p. 222), while the Roman slaves were just prosperous enough for its pursuit (p. 113).

known least of all to the discoverer, whose knowledge of technology is mostly slight—all this is overcome by the assumption that social needs compel discoveries which scientists believe to flow from the internal logic of scientific development. Thus they are supposed unconsciously to follow a practical purpose of which they are themselves unaware. Crowther explains, for example, the course taken by Clerk-Maxwell when embarking (around 1855) on his studies of the theory of gases and of the electric field, as follows:

> Mercantilism had surrendered the initiative to industrialism, and navigation gave place to the steam engine and the telegraph. In parallel with this social movement, mathematical astronomy gave place to heat and electricity . . . Maxwell's reform appeared to him mainly as a transfer of attention to those parts of science that seemed most promising of important discovery. He did not inquire why heat and electricity appeared to him more promising than astronomy. It was sufficient that he knew that they were so. History has entirely confirmed Maxwell's opinion, though he regarded it as self-evident. It is possible now to see that he was an intellectual instrument of a development determined by the main social forces of his time, while his choice of studies appeared to himself to be determined by the logic of their own development.[8]

Mr. Crowther's theory of Maxwell's position in the midst of the industrial interests surrounding him is up to a point analogous to the well-known type of demagogical construction: "The Jews desire Hitler's fall; Churchill fights Hitler; hence Churchill is the tool of the Jews." The difference is only that Mr. Crowther's construction contains one more element of magical reasoning. In his argument there is no question of the tool (Maxwell) being actually intent on promoting the interests in question; it is admitted that he was not aware of future practical applications of his work. Thus

8. J. G. Crowther, loc. cit., p. 453.

Maxwell becomes an *unconscious* tool of interests, to which he was admittedly indifferent, in the pursuit of future results, of which he was admittedly ignorant. Such constructions gain strength in the eyes of their believers from the very fact of their absurdity; for the absence of tangible reality is taken to prove the presence of a profound, hidden principle of "social determinism."

A common manifestation of the same fallacious intellectual instinct, which Mr. Crowther utilizes in this argument, appears in the irresistible habit of the beginner—so often reproved in schools—to "write history backwards." The novice keeps reconstructing the minds of people at an earlier period of time as if they could have known the events which followed in a later period. It requires a trained effort of the imagination to avoid infusing the minds of historic characters with a foreknowledge of their own future, which forms an integral part of our present conception of them.

The writing of history backwards is a standard method for proving the magic powers of social needs in directing the discoveries of scientists. Professor Hogben applies it as follows to the case of Maxwell:

> . . . in Maxwell's treatise the Newtonian mathematics of the older universities was linked to the experimental measurements made by Faraday and Henry in extra-mural foundations, such as the Royal and Smithsonian Institutions. As with the form, so it was with the substance. From the beginnings of practical telegraphy the possibility of propagating electrical phenomena through space without the aid of conducting material in the ordinary sense continually prompted speculation and experiment. In the adventurous hopefulness of nineteenth-century industrialism, telegraphy without wires was the philosopher's stone and the elixir of youth. Thus far, telegraphic communication was the most spectacular achievement of science. As such it received its full share of recognition in the Great Exhibition which coincided

with the Atlantic Cable venture. Two years later—in 1853—Dering, an inventor whose electrical appliances received an honourable place among the exhibits, referred to the "craving there is at present for wireless telegraphs." This was the year in which Maxwell became second wrangler.[9]

Fantastic exaggerations ("philosopher's stone," "elixir of youth"), referring to a problem which it would be more correct to describe as an obscure one at the time in question,[10] together with other colourful stage settings, thus endow the method of writing history backwards with irresistible power; in particular when the subject is one known to few, and the writings are addressed to the general public in combination with a political message which they convey.

To make the position thus established impregnable, it is only necessary to keep it sufficiently obscure. Strictly speak-

9. *Science for the Citizen,* p. 737.

10. The urgent need of wireless transmission arose, according to Professor Hogben, from a burning desire to save the cost of telegraphic cables. The actual state of affairs can be assessed as follows. Owing to various technical difficulties, wireless transmission has never superseded cable telegraphy. On the land the use of cable remains uncontested and the competition between wireless and cable for overseas telegraphy is yet undecided. This fact, far from moving all scientific speculations of our time, remains unmentioned even by the author of *Science for the Citizen,* who takes such particular interest in the problem.

The real importance of wireless transmission (apart from its more recent application to broadcasting) has obviously been in the field of navigation—the supposed loss of interest in which is thought (by Mr. Crowther) to have turned Maxwell's mind from astronomy to electric waves. Actually, to-day, this country depends for its very life on navigation; and this dependence arose precisely in the decades after the repeal of the Corn Laws: in Maxwell's time. Thus a flippant critic might suggest that the theory of social determinism has proved right after all—only that Maxwell's response was not to the decline, but rather to the sudden increase in the national significance of navigation.

ing *no definite statement whatever* has been made above by Professor Hogben about the reasons that led Maxwell to develop the theory of electromagnetic waves, which about half a century later contributed to the invention of wireless telegraphy. At least none that would go beyond the commonly held and rather irrelevant opinion, that the study of electricity in the nineteenth century gained added interest from its wide practical applications. Yet the force of indirect suggestion in Professor Hogben's quoted passage is so strong that he can use it to prove his attack—made on the page before—on the view generally accepted in previous literature, that Maxwell "laboured for knowledge alone" and was justified in doing so. This—we are told by Professor Hogben—is nothing but an "arrogant pretence" of scientists.

The remarkable fact that this new theory of science is always demonstrated by examples of a comparatively remote past, *in the midst of our century possessing unparalleled scientific achievements of its own,* can be understood from the above analysis. The practical applications of recent discoveries are not yet known, so that in their case history cannot yet be written backwards. What technical inventions were the discoveries of the Nobel Laureates Planck, Einstein, Perrin, Millikan, Michelson, Rutherford, Aston, Chadwick, Barkla, Heisenberg, Compton, Franck, G. Hertz, Rubens, Laue, Joliot, Fermi, Urey, Anderson, W. H. and W. L. Bragg, Schrödinger, Dirac, etc., unconsciously intended to produce? No one can tell—so the new theory of science must pass them over.

One wonders how the great physicists in the list above would have fared if, before embarking on their investigation, they had had to get a certificate of its social usefulness from a scientific directorate, as contemplated by Marxist scientists and their friends. To what conflicts may not have led their "arrogant pretence" to be sole judges of their own preference!

V

But we are told that the planning of science is actually in successful operation in the Soviet Union. What is the truth in this matter? How does the planning of science operate in the Soviet Union? Briefly, the position is this. There have been set up in Russia rather extensive laboratories for applied research. Their purpose is to promote various forms of practical science on lines similar to those followed by their counterparts in Britain, America, etc. There is nothing distinctive about these activities except the idea of calling them "planned science." To this, however, we must add a somewhat more serious feature. There is a good deal of talk in Russia about detailed plans for research in each laboratory, and also about the planning of pure research with a view to the benefit of industry. Fortunately this "planning" has remained almost entirely on paper. It is true that you may read descriptions such as that by Mr. J. G. Crowther on the planning of scientific work in the laboratory of Physics in Kharkov: "Each department [says Crowther] draws up a plan for work from January 1st to December 31st of each year. The plan is given in detail for each quarter, and there must even be a suggestion of what will be done each day. At the end of each month the research worker assesses what percentage he has accomplished of his plan. This is usually about 80 per cent. to 90 per cent., and the assessments are notably honest"[11] (which is about as reasonable as planning a test match by fixing in advance the scores of each player on both sides). But the truth in such cases is merely that the Soviet scientists were made to fill in a lot of meaningless forms. Even though in a number of instances (particularly

11. *Manchester Guardian Commercial*, 2nd June, 1934.

in psychology and in genetics) there has been some serious interference with the integrity of science, a good deal of scientific research continues to be done in Russia in exactly the same way as everywhere else. Research continues to advance on the lines of the universal system of science and the Russian pieces fit in with the British, the Swiss and the Japanese pieces, as well as with other pieces from all over the world.

Recently, evidence has reached us that Soviet scientists are trying to shake off the imposition of Marxist theories on the valuation and organization of science. In an important speech made in 1943 to the Presidium of the Soviet Academy, Academician Kapitza advocated that each research institute of the Academy should be devoted to a particular branch of what he called "great science," but what from the context clearly appears to be our old friend, fundamental or pure science.[12] Research (we are told) should be conducted with a view to the best success that can be achieved in its own branch of science. "The direction in which the institute develops must correspond to that direction of this science which is most promising at the moment, and which, taking into consideration the present state of science and the methodological possibilities, has the widest prospects for rapid and fruitful progress." That is exactly the way systematic science has advanced in the past everywhere. Science, Kapitza declares accordingly, forms a unity all over the world in all countries, regardless, it would seem, of their social system of production. And as regards the relations of pure science to applied science he says that ". . . it

12. I am indebted to the Society for the Cultural Relations with the U.S.S.R., for the loan of a detailed report of this meeting. A brief extract appeared in *Nature*, vol. 155 (1945), p. 294.

is not right to insist that a scientist should seek the application of his scientific work to industry." As regards planning, he demands that ". . . a scientific institute should have a very flexible organization. Indeed, in the course of creative work it is difficult to look even one month ahead, let alone a year." Kapitza's speech was greeted by his distinguished audience with signs of relief and broad approval; it is clear that a new departure was made at this meeting.[13]

Thus the new strictly utilitarian valuation of science and the attempt at planning science may be abandoned in the country of their first origin. It seems possible also that the movement in Britain which has run parallel to the earlier tendencies of Soviet Russia will then be gradually slackened. In fact, the recent utterances of the usual advocates of planned science show definite signs in this direction.

Shall we, then, regard, the whole interlude as virtually closed and expect the position of science to return in effect to what it was before? I hardly think so. The extravagant idea of subordinating science to the planning of welfare has formed but one part of a general attack on the status of intellectual and moral life. There are a number of important movements to-day denying the ultimate reality of rational and moral processes. A vast force of naturalistic prejudice is relentlessly attacking the conception of man as an essentially rational being.

In this *milieu*, science as a pure search for truth can hardly be expected to regain the respect which it previously enjoyed. While such forces prevail, society is unlikely to re-

13. At the date of collecting my essays into this volume (November 1949) it appears that the expectations raised by Kapitza's speech never materialized. Instead, references to Kapitza have gradually vanished from the Soviet press and for the past three years or so he has completely disappeared from the public eye. The brief relaxation of Marxist policy was followed by a rapidly increasing harshness of its application up to the present day.

gard itself as dedicated to the continued cultivation of an intellectual heritage, to which each generation can add but little. On the contrary, the tendency will remain for the State to claim ultimate responsibility for every activity affecting the welfare of its citizens, including the progress of science. I see no reason to assume that the crisis of our civilization evoked by this fundamental tendency has as yet reached its ultimate climax.

6

Planned Science[1]

This age of ours has had its great revolutionary movements, but it also staged some strange wild-goose chases. About ten years ago there suddenly arose in Britain a movement for the planning of science. The books which spread this new doctrine became best-sellers and they attracted a great number of followers. Their forces foregathered in a new division of the British Association founded in 1938. The movement penetrated widely into the masses of scientifically trained people through the Association of Scientific Workers which expanded under this impetus to a membership of over 15,000. In January 1943 the Association held a crowded conference in London which was presided over by Sir Robert Watson Watt, and filled the Caxton Hall to overflowing. Sponsors and speakers included some of the most eminent scientists in Britain. It was taken for granted from the start that all scientific work must be integrated under the guidance of planning boards on the model of those established in wartime. Speaker after speaker condemned in angry and

1. Broadcast, Sept., 1948.

106

sweeping terms the traditional modes of conducting scientific activities, and a detailed description of Russian planning went uncriticized. Professor Bernal declared that in the wartime organization of science "we had learned for the first time how to carry on scientific work rapidly and effectively."

No opposing voices were heard at the conference, and anti-planners were castigated as people agitating for anarchy and ignorance. It really seemed that in Britain the movement for the planning of science was rushing forward irresistibly to victory. And yet to-day one can hardly remember what it was all about. The demand for a central planning of science is almost forgotten. The books which started the movement for planning are still read, but their message is no longer taken seriously. The movement has petered out, leaving hardly a trace. If you compare for example the post-war development of scientific organization in Britain with that of America, where there has never been a planning movement, there is no difference that could be ascribed to the movement for planning. In the universities of both countries scientific research continues substantially on traditional lines.

The whole curious interlude could, in fact, be now forgotten and left for the future historian to ponder on, but for two vital reasons: first, there is the fact that our fellow-scientists in Russia have still to submit to regimentation by planning, or at least have to waste their time and surrender the dignity of their calling by pretending to submit to it. Worse still, they remain constantly in danger of falling victim to the machinations of political careerists: men who gain influence in science by pretending to be the fulfillers of Marxism and who may at any moment direct against their fellow-scientists the deadly shafts of Marxian suspicion and Marxian invective. The fate of Vavilov and of his many collaborators who succumbed to the "planning of science" as exercised by Lysenko, can never be absent from the thoughts of any Russian scientist. It falls to us to fight the false and oppressive doctrine forced upon our Russian colleagues, which, even while they are bitterly suffering under it, they are compelled to support in public.

And then, though the movement for the planning of science has been without effect in Britain, it remains no less a disturbing symptom of the instability of our days. It should remind us that in this present revolutionary period, no great institution can take its own continued acceptance for granted, for even the most ancient and well-founded claims are at such times in danger of going by default if left undefended. Before the controversy over the planning of science, there had been little attempt made to examine closely either the principles by which scientific progress is achieved, or the policies which have customarily guided the organization of science. Now that we have had our warning, we must clearly recognize where we stand in these matters. Henceforth we must be able to declare explicitly what our fundamental principles are and to vindicate them in the face of new problems and new hostile doctrines.

The traditional claim that scientific research can be effectively pursued only by independent scientists can be traced back to the earliest statement of freedom of thought by Milton in his *Areopagitica*. Yet the belief that science can prosper only in freedom may seem to conflict with the accepted definition of science as systematic knowledge. How can a structure which claims to be systematic prosper from additions made by individuals without any central guidance? Suppose we started building a house without any plans, each workman adding his part according to his own ideas, using whatever materials he preferred, putting in bricks or timber, lead pipes or floorboards as he thought fit. Surely the result would be a hopeless confusion.

If science really does prosper by allowing each scientist to follow his own bent, the systematic structure of science must differ fundamentally from that which underlies the structure of a house. And this is quite true. The nature of scientific systems is more akin to the ordered arrangement of living cells which constitute a polycellular organism. The progress of science through the individual efforts of independent scientists is comparable in many ways to the growth of a higher organism from a single microscopic germ-cell. Throughout the process of embryonic development each cell pursues its own life, and yet each so adjusts its growth to that of its neighbours that a harmonious structure of the aggregate emerges. This is exactly how scientists co-operate: by continually adjusting their line of research to the results achieved up to date by their fellow-scientists.

However, just as science cannot be planned by men as they plan a house, neither do scientists form part of science in the way cells form part of an organism. The actual situation, which lies somewhere between the two, may perhaps be better pictured by using Milton's simile, which likens truth to a shattered statue, with fragments lying widely scattered and hidden in many places. Each scientist on his own initiative pursues independently the task of finding one fragment of the statue and fitting it to those collected by others. This explains well enough the manner in which free scientists jointly pursue a single systematic purpose.

But there is another feature of science which is of great importance for its correct organization and does not fit in so readily with this picture. The progressive stages of scientific knowledge have a deceptive completeness which makes them resemble more the developing shapes of a growing organism than the mutilated forms of an incomplete statue. If we pieced together a statue and there was no head to it, we should feel sure that it was yet incomplete. But science in its progress does not appear obviously incomplete even though large parts of it may still be missing. Physics as it stood half a century ago, though lacking quantum theory and relativity, and ignorant of electrons and radioactivity, was yet thought at the time to be essentially complete; and not only by laymen, but also by the scientific authorities of the time. To illustrate the growth of science we must imagine a statue which, while it is being pieced together, appears complete at every successive stage. And we may add that it would also appear to change its meaning on the addition of every successive fragment—to the great and ever renewed surprise of the bystanders.

And here indeed emerges the decisive reason for individualism in the cultivation of science. No committee of scientists, however distinguished, could forecast the further progress of science except for the routine extension of the existing system. No important scientific advance could ever be foretold by such a committee. The problems allocated by it would therefore be of no real scientific value. They would either be devoid of originality, or if, throwing prudence to the winds, the committee once ventured on some really novel proposals, their suggestions would invariably prove impracticable. For the points at which the existing system of science can be effectively amended reveal themselves only to the individual investigator. And even he can discover only through a lifelong concentration on one particular aspect of science a small number of practicable and really worth-while problems.

The pursuit of science can be organized, therefore, in no other manner than by granting complete independence to all mature scientists. They will then distribute themselves over the whole field of possible discoveries, each applying his own special ability to the task that appears most profitable to him. Thus as many trails as possible will be covered, and science will penetrate most rapidly in every direction towards that kind of hidden knowledge which is unsuspected by all but its discoverer, the kind of new knowledge on which the progress of science truly depends. The function of public authorities is not to plan research, but only to provide opportunities for its pursuit. All that they have to do is to provide facilities for every good scientist to follow his own interests in science. To do less is to neglect the progress of science; to do more is to cultivate mediocrity and waste public money. Such principles have in fact essentially guided all well-conducted universities throughout the modern age.

Apart from opportunities for research, there must facilities for the publication of new discoveries; or, more precisely, of all claims to new discoveries. That involves a problem. We must guard against cranks and frauds, and also keep out ordinary blunderers, if scientific journals are not to spread confusion. Yet the work of pioneers which at first sight may look unsound and sometimes even crazy, must not be excluded. Similar problems have to be met in the selection of personnel for scientific appointments and in the allocation of funds. Herein lies the vital control of scientific life. The responsibility for operating it rests, ultimately, with organized scientific opinion. It has to act as a policeman the year round and yet ever remain on the alert, to offer its help to the true revolutionary—the creative breaker of the law. To guard scientific standards, while assuring full scope to new heterodox talent, is the function of scientific opinion. For this it needs humility in the service of science. But it must also take pride in that which it serves and demand respect for it everywhere. For science is not the don's fad or the student's grind, but a way of understanding nature, equally needful to every man.

PART II

Other Examples

7

Perils of Inconsistency

This chapter is about intellectual freedom. I shall argue that its doctrine, as handed down to us, is intrinsically inconsistent and that the fall of liberty on the Continent of Europe was an outcome of this inadequacy. Freedom of thought destroyed itself when a self-contradictory conception of liberty was pursued to its ultimate conclusions.

To present this argument, I must glance back for a moment to the very beginning of systematic thinking. Modern thought in the widest sense emerged with the emancipation of the human mind from a mythological and magical interpretation of the universe. We know when this first happened, at what place and by what method. This act of liberation was due to the Ionian philosophers who flourished in the sixth century B.C. They were succeeded by other philosophers of Greece covering a period of a thousand years. These ancient thinkers enjoyed much freedom of speculation without ever raising decisively the issues of intellectual freedom.

The millennium of ancient philosophy was brought to a close by St. Augustine. There followed the long rule of Christian theology and the Church of Rome over all departments of thought. The rule of ecclesiastic authority was first impaired from the twelfth century on by a number of sporadic intellectual achievements. Then, as the Italian Renaissance blossomed out, the leading artists and thinkers of the time brought religion more and more into neglect. The Italian Church itself seemed to yield to the new secular interests. Had the whole of Europe been at the time of the same mind as Italy, Renaissance Humanism might have established freedom of thought everywhere, simply by default of opposition. Europe might have returned to—or if you like relapsed into—a liberalism resembling that of pre-Christian antiquity. Whatever may have followed after that, our present disasters would not have occurred.

However, there arose instead in a number of European countries, in Germany, Switzerland, Spain, a fervent religious revival, accompanied by a schism of the Christian churches, which was to dominate people's minds for almost two centuries. The Catholic Church sharply re-affirmed its authority over the whole intellectual sphere. The thoughts of men were moved and politics shaped by the struggle between Protestantism and Catholicism, to which all contemporary issues contributed by alliance to one side or the other.

By the beginning of the present century—to which I am leading up now—the wars between Catholics and Protestants had long ceased; yet the formulation of liberal thought still remained largely determined by the reaction of past generations against the period of religious wars. Liberalism was motivated, to start with, by detestation of religious fanaticism. It appealed to reason for a cessation of religious strife. This desire to curb religious violence was the prime motive of liberalism both in the Anglo-American and in the Continental area. Yet from the beginning the reaction against religious fanaticism differed somewhat in these two areas, and this difference has since become increasingly accentuated, so that in consequence liberty was upheld in the Western area up to this day and suffered a collapse in the territories of Central and Eastern Europe.

Anglo-American liberalism was first formulated by Milton and Locke. Their argument for freedom of thought was twofold. In its first part (for which we may quote the *Areopagitica*) freedom from authority is demanded, so that truth may be discovered. The main inspiration of this movement was the struggle of the rising natural sciences against the authority of Aristotle. Its programme was to let everyone state his beliefs, and to allow people to listen and form their own opinion; the ideas which would prevail in a free and open battle of wits would be as close an approximation to the truth as can be humanly achieved. We may call this the anti-authoritarian formula of liberty. Closely related to it is the second half of the argument for liberty, which is based on philosophic doubt. While its origins go back a long way (right to the philosophers of antiquity) this argument was first formulated as a political doctrine by Locke. It says simply that we can never be so sure of the truth in matters of religion as to warrant the imposition of our views on others. These two pleas for freedom of thought were put forward and were accepted by England at a time when religious beliefs were unshaken and indeed dominant throughout the nation. The new tolerance aimed pre-eminently at the reconciliation of different denominations in the service of God. Atheists were refused tolerance by Locke, as socially unreliable.

On the Continent, the twofold doctrine of free thought —anti-authoritarianism and philosophic doubt—gained ascendancy somewhat later than in England and moved on straightaway to a more extreme position. This was first effectively formulated in the eighteenth century by the philosophy of Enlightenment, which was primarily an attack on religious authority and particularly on the Catholic Church.

It professed a radical scepticism. The books of Voltaire and of the French Encyclopaedists expounding this doctrine were widely read in France, while abroad their ideas spread into Germany and far into Eastern Europe. Frederick the Great and Catherine of Russia were among their correspondents and disciples. The type of Voltairian aristocrat, represented by the old Prince Bolkonski in *War and Peace*, was to be found at Court and in feudal residences over many parts of Continental Europe at the close of the eighteenth century. The depth to which the philosophers had influenced political thought in their own country was to be revealed by the French Revolution.

Accordingly, the mood of French Enlightenment, though often angry, was always supremely confident. Its followers promised to mankind relief from all social ills. One of the central figures of the movement, the Baron d'Holbach, declared this in his *Systeme de la Nature* (1770) as follows:

"Man is miserable, simply because he is ignorant. His mind is so infected with prejudices, that one might think him for ever condemned to err. . . . It is error that has evoked the religious fears, which shrivel up men with fright, or make them butcher each other for chimeras. The hatred, persecutions, massacres and tragedies of which, under the pretexts of the interests of Heaven, the earth has been the repeated theatre, are one and all the outcome of error."

This explanation of human miseries and the remedy which is promised for them continued to carry conviction to the intelligentsia of Europe long after the French Revolution. It remained an axiom among progressive people on the Continent that to achieve light and liberty, you had first to break the power of the clergy and eliminate the influence of religious dogma. Battle after battle was fought in this campaign. Perhaps the fiercest engagement was that about the Dreyfus affair at the close of the century, in which clericalism was finally defeated in France, and further weakened throughout Europe. It was about this time that W. E. H. Lecky wrote in his *History of Rationalism in Europe* (1893): "All over Europe the priesthood are now associated with a policy of toryism, of reaction or of obstruction. All over Europe the organs that represent dogmatic interests are in permanent opposition to the progressive tendencies around them, and are rapidly sinking into contempt."

I well remember this triumphant sentiment. We looked back on earlier times as on a period of darkness, and with Lucretius we cried in horror: *"Tantum religio potuit suadere malorum";* what evils religion had inspired! So we rejoiced at the superior knowledge of our age and its assured liberties. The promises of peace and freedom given to the world by French Enlightenment had indeed been wonderfully fulfilled toward the end of the nineteenth century. You could travel all over Europe and America without a passport and settle down wherever you pleased. With the exception of Russia, you could print throughout Europe anything without previous censorship and could sharply oppose any government or creed, with impunity. In Germany—much criticized at the time for being authoritarian—biting caricatures of the Emperor were published freely. Even in Russia, whose regime was most oppressive, Marx's *Kapital* appeared in translation immediately after its first publication and received favourable reviews throughout the press. In the whole of Europe not more than a few hundred people were forced into political exile. Throughout the planet all men of European race were living in free intellectual and personal communication. It is hardly surprising that the universal establishment of peace and tolerance through the victory of modern enlightenment, was confidently expected at the turn of the century by a large majority of educated people on the Continent of Europe.

Thus we entered on the twentieth century as on an age of infinite promise. Few people realized at the time that we were walking into a minefield—even though the mines had all been prepared and carefully laid in open daylight by well-known thinkers of our own age. To-day we know that our expectations proved false. We have all learned to trace the collapse of freedom in the twentieth century to the writings of certain philosophers, particularly of Marx, Nietzsche, and their common ancestors, Fichte and Hegel. But the story has yet to be told how we came to welcome as liberators the philosophies which were to destroy liberty.

I have said that I consider the collapse of freedom in Central and Eastern Europe as the outcome of an internal contradiction in the doctrine of liberty. Wherein lies this inconsistency? Why did it destroy freedom in large parts of Continental Europe, and has not had similar effects so far in the Western or Anglo-American area of our civilization?

The argument of doubt put forward by Locke in favour of tolerance says that since it is impossible to demonstrate which religion is true, we should admit them all. This implies that we must not impose beliefs that are not demonstrable. Let us apply this doctrine to ethical principles. It follows that unless ethical principles can be demonstrated with certainty, we should refrain from imposing them and should tolerate their total denial. But of course, ethical principles cannot be demonstrated: you cannot prove the obligation to tell the truth, to uphold justice and mercy. It would follow therefore that a system of mendacity, lawlessness and cruelty is to be accepted as an alternative to ethical principles on equal terms. But a society in which unscrupulous propaganda, violence and terror prevail offers no scope for tolerance. Here the inconsistency of a liberalism based on philosophic doubt becomes apparent: freedom of thought is destroyed by the extension of doubt to the field of traditional ideals.

The consummation of this destructive process was prevented in the Anglo-American region by an instinctive reluctance to pursue the accepted philosophic premises to their ultimate conclusions. One way of avoiding this was by pretending that ethical principles could actually be scientifically demonstrated. Locke himself started this train of thought by asserting that good and evil could be identified with pleasure and pain, and suggesting that all ideals of good behaviour are merely maxims of prudence.

However, the utilitarian calculus cannot in fact demonstrate our obligations to ideals which demand serious sacrifices from us. A man's sincerity in professing his ideals is to be measured rather by the *lack* of prudence which he shows in pursuing them. The utilitarian confirmation of unselfishness is no more than a pretence, by which traditional ideals are made acceptable to a philosophically sceptical age. Camouflaged as long-term selfishness, the traditional ideals of man are protected from destruction by scepticism.

I believe that the preservation up to this day of Western civilization along the lines of the Anglo-American tradition of liberty was due to this speculative restraint, amounting to a veritable suspension of logic within the British empiricist philosophy. It was enough to pay philosophic lip-service to the supremacy of the pleasure-principle. Ethical standards were not really replaced by new purposes; still less was there any inclination of abandoning these standards in practice. The masses of the people and their leaders in public life could in fact disregard the accepted philosophy, both in deciding their personal conduct and in building up their political institutions. The whole sweeping advance of moral aspirations to which the Age of Reason opened the way—the English Revolution, the American Revolution, the French

Revolution, the first liberation of the slaves in the British Empire, the Factory Reforms, the founding of the League of Nations, Britain's stand against Hitler, the offering of Lend-Lease, U.N.R.R.A. and Marshall Aid, the sending of millions of food parcels by individual Americans to unknown beneficiaries in Europe—in all these decisive actions public opinion was swayed by moral forces, by charity, by a desire for justice and a detestation of social evils which disregarded the fact that these had no true justification in the prevailing philosophy of the age. Utilitarianism and other allied materialistic formulations of traditional ideals remained on paper. The philosophic impairment of universal moral standards led only to their verbal replacement; it was a sham-replacement, or to give it a technical designation, we may speak of a "pseudo-substitution" of utilitarian purposes for moral principles.

The speculative and practical restraints which saved liberalism from self-destruction in the Anglo-American area were due in the first place to the distinctly religious character of this liberalism. So long as philosophic doubt was applied only in order to secure equal rights to all religions and was prohibited from demanding equal rights also for irreligion, the same restraint would automatically apply in respect to moral beliefs. A scepticism which was kept on short leash for the sake of preserving religious beliefs, would hardly become a menace to fundamental moral principles. A second restraint on scepticism, closely related to the first, lay in the establishment of democratic institutions at a time when religious beliefs were still strong. These institutions (for example the American Constitution) gave effect to the moral principles which underlie a free society. The tradition of democracy embodied in these institutions proved strong enough to uphold in practice the moral standards of a free society against any critique which would question their validity.

Both these protective restraints, however, were absent in those parts of Europe where liberalism was based on French Enlightenment. This movement being anti-religious, it imposed no restraint on sceptical speculations; nor were the standards of morality embodied here in democratic institutions. When a feudal society, dominated by religious authority, was attacked by a radical scepticism, there emerged a liberalism which was unprotected either by a religious or a civic tradition against destruction by the philosophic scepticism to which it owed its origin.

Let me describe briefly what happened. From the middle of the eighteenth century, Continental thought faced up seriously to the fact that the universal standards of reason could not be philosophically justified in the light of the sceptical attitude which had initiated the rationalist movement. The great philosophic tumult which started in the second half of the eighteenth century on the Continent of Europe and which finally led up to the philosophic disasters of our own days, represented an incessant preoccupation with the collapse of the philosophic foundations of rationalism. Universal standards of human behaviour having fallen into philosophic disrepute, various substitutes were put forward in their place. I shall indicate the main forms under which these made their appearance.

The first kind of substitute standard was derived from the contemplation of individuality. The case for the uniqueness of the individual is set out as follows in the opening words of Rousseau's *Confessions*. He talks about himself: "Myself alone. . . . There is no one who resembles me. . . . We shall see whether Nature was right in breaking the mould into which she had cast me." Individuality here challenged the world to judge it, if it can, by universal standards. Creative genius claimed to be the renewer of all values and therefore to be incommensurable. This claim was to be extended to whole nations; according to it, each nation had its unique set of values which could not be validly criticized in the light of universal reason. A nation's only obligation was, like that of the unique individual, to realize its own powers. In following the call of its destiny, a nation must allow no other nation to stand in its way.

If you apply this claim for the supremacy of uniqueness —which we may call Romanticism—to single persons, you arrive at a general hostility to society, as exemplified in the anti-conventional and almost extra-territorial attitude of the Continental bohème. If applied to nations, it results on the contrary in the conception of a unique national destiny which claims the absolute allegiance of all its citizens. The national leader combines the advantages of both. He can stand entranced in the admiration of his own uniqueness, while identifying his personal ambitions with the destiny of the nation lying at his feet.

Romanticism was a literary movement and a change of heart, rather than a philosophy. Its counterpart in systematic thought was constructed by the Hegelian dialectic. Hegel took charge of Universal Reason, emaciated to a ghost by its treatment at the hands of Kant, and clad it with the warm flesh of history. Declared incompetent to judge historic action, reason was given the comfortable position of being immanent in history. An ideal situation: "Heads you lose, tails I win." Identified with the stronger battalions, reason became invincible; but unfortunately also redundant.

The next step was therefore quite naturally the complete disestablishment of reason. Marx and Engels decided to turn the Hegelian dialectic right way up. No longer should the tail pretend to wag the dog. The bigger battalions should be recognized as makers of history in their own right, with reason as a mere apologist to justify their conquests.

The story of this last development is well known. Marx reinterpreted history as the outcome of class conflicts, which arise from the need of adjusting "the relations of production" to "the forces of production." Expressed in ordinary language this says that as new technical equipment becomes available from time to time, it is necessary to change the order of property in favour of a new class, which is invariably achieved by overthrowing the hitherto favoured class. Socialism, it was said, brings these violent changes to a close by establishing the classless society. From its first formulation in the *Communist Manifesto* this doctrine places the "eternal truths, such as Freedom, Justice, etc."—which it mentions in these terms—into a very doubtful position. Since these ideas are supposed to have always been used only to soothe the conscience of the rulers and bemuse the suspicions of the exploited, there is no clear place left for them in the classless society. To-day it has become apparent that there is indeed nothing in the realm of ideas, from law and religion to poetry and science, from the rules of football to the composition of music, that cannot be readily interpreted by Marxists as a mere product of class interest.

Meanwhile the legacy of Romantic nationalism, developing on parallel lines, was also gradually transposed into materialistic terms. Wagner and the Walhalla no doubt affected Nazi imagery; Mussolini gloried in recalling Imperial Rome. But the really effective idea of Hitler and Mussolini was their classification of nations into *haves* and *have-nots* on the model of Marxian class-war. The actions of nations were in this view not determined, nor capable of being judged by right or wrong. Those in possession preached peace and the sacredness of international law, since the law sanctioned their holdings. But of course this code was unacceptable to virile nations, left empty-handed; they would rise and overthrow the degenerate capitalistic democracies which had become the dupes of their pacific ideology, originally intended only to bemuse the underdogs. And so the text of Fascist and National-socialist foreign policy ran on, exactly on the lines of a Marxism applied to class war between nations. Indeed, already by the opening of the twentieth century, influential German writers had fully refashioned the nationalism of Fichte and Hegel on the lines of a power-political interpretation of history. Romanticism had been brutalized and brutality romanticized, until the product was as tough as Marx's own historic materialism.

We have here the final outcome of the Continental cycle of thought. The self-destruction of Liberalism, which was kept in a state of suspended logic in the Anglo-American field of Western civilization, was here brought to its ultimate conclusion. The process of replacing moral ideals by philosophically less vulnerable objectives was carried out in all seriousness. This is not a mere pseudo-substitution, but a *real* substitution of human appetites and human passions for reason and the ideals of man.

This brings us right up to the scene of the revolutions of the twentieth century. We can see now how the philosophies which guided these revolutions and destroyed liberty wherever they prevailed, were originally justified by the anti-authoritarian and sceptical formula of liberty. They were indeed anti-authoritarian and sceptical to the extreme. They set man free from obligations towards truth and justice, reducing reason to its own caricature: to a mere rationalization of conclusions, pre-determined by desire and eventually to be secured, or already held, by force. Such was the final measure of this liberation: man was to be recognized henceforth as maker and master, and no longer servant of what had before been his ideals.

This liberation, however, destroyed the very foundations of liberty. If thought and reason are nothing by themselves, then it is meaningless to demand that thought be set free.

The boundless hopes which the Enlightenment of the eighteenth century attached to the overthrow of authority and to the pursuit of doubt, were hopes attached to the release of reason. Its followers firmly believed—to use Jefferson's majestic vocabulary—in "truths that are self-evident," which would guard "life, liberty and the pursuit of happiness," under governments "deriving their just powers from the consent of the governed." They relied on truths, which they trusted to be inscribed in the hearts of men, for establishing peace and freedom among men everywhere. The assumption of universal standards of reason was implicit in the hopes of Enlightenment and the philosophies which denied the existence of such standards denied therefore the foundations of all these hopes.

But it is not enough to show how a logical process, starting from an inadequate formulation of liberty, led to philosophic conclusions that contradicted liberty. I have yet to show that this contradiction was actually put into operation; that these conclusions were not merely entertained and believed to be true, but met people prepared to act upon them. If ideas cause revolutions, they can only do so through people who will act upon them. If my account of the fall of liberty in Europe is to satisfy you, I must be able to show that there were people who actually transformed philosophic error into destructive human action.

Of such people we have ample documentary evidence among the intelligentsia of Central and Eastern Europe. We may describe them as Nihilists.

There is an interesting ambiguity in the connotations of the word "nihilism," which at first may seem confusing, but actually turns out to be illuminating. Remember Rauschning's interpretation of the National Socialist upheaval in his book *Germany's Revolution of Nihilism*. As against this, reports

127

from Central Europe often speak of widespread nihilism, meaning a lack of public spirit, the apathy of people who believe in nothing. This curious duality of nihilism, which makes it a by-word both for complete self-centredness and violent revolutionary action, can be traced to its earliest origins. The word was popularized by Turgenev in his *Fathers and Sons,* written in 1862. His prototype of nihilism, the student Bazarov, is an extreme individualist without any interest in politics. Nor does the next similar figure of Russian literature, Dostoevski's Raskolnikov in *Crime and Punishment* (1865), show any political leanings. What Raskolnikov is trying to find out is why he should not murder an old woman, if he wanted her money. Both Bazarov and Raskolnikov are experimenting privately with a life of total disbelief. But already a few years later we see the nihilist transformed into a political conspirator. The terrorist organization of the Narodniki—or Populists—had come into being. Dostoevski portrayed the new type in his later novel, *The Possessed.* The nihilist now appears as an ice-cold businesslike conspirator, closely prefiguring the ideal Bolshevik as I have seen him represented on the Moscow stage in the didactic plays of the early Stalin period. Nor is the similarity accidental. For the whole code of conspiratorial action—the cells, the secrecy, the discipline and ruthlessness—known as the Communist method to-day, was taken over by Lenin from the "Populists"; proof of which can be found in articles published by him in 1901.

English and American people find it difficult to understand nihilism, for most of the doctrines professed by nihilists have been current among themselves for some time without turning those who held them into nihilists. Great solid Bentham would not have disagreed with any of the views expounded by Turgenev's prototype of nihilism, the student Bazarov. But while Bentham and other sceptically minded Englishmen may use such philosophies merely as a mistaken explanation of their own conduct, which in actual fact is determined by their traditional beliefs—the nihilist Bazarov and his kind take such philosophies seriously and try to live by their light.

The nihilist who tries to live without any beliefs, obligations, or restrictions, stands at the first, the private stage of nihilism. He is represented in Russia by the earlier type of intellectual described by Turgenev and the younger Dostoevski. In Germany we find nihilists of this kind growing up in large numbers under the influence of Nietzsche and Stirner; and later, between 1910 and 1930, we see emerging in direct line of their succession the great German Youth Movement, with its radical contempt for all existing social ties.

But the solitary nihilist is unstable. Starved of social responsibility, he is liable to be drawn into politics, provided he can find a movement based on nihilistic assumptions. Thus, when he turns to public affairs, he adopts a creed of political violence. The cafés of Munich, Berlin, Vienna, Prague, and Budapest, where writers, painters, lawyers, doctors, had spent so many hours of amusing speculation and gossip, thus became in 1918 the recruiting grounds for the "armed bohémians," whom Heiden in his book on Hitler describes as the agents of the European Revolution. Just as the Bloomsbury of the unbridled twenties unexpectedly turned out numerous disciplined Marxists around 1930.

The conversion of the nihilist from extreme individualism to the service of a fierce and narrow political creed is the turning-point of the European Revolution. The downfall of liberty in Europe consisted in a series of such individual conversions.

Their mechanism deserves closest attention. Take first conversion to Marxism. Historic materialism had all the attractions of a second Enlightenment—taking off and carrying on from the first anti-religious Enlightenment, and offering the same intense mental satisfaction. Those who accepted its guidance felt suddenly initiated to the real forces actuating men and operating in history; to a reality that had hitherto been hidden to them and still remained hidden to the unenlightened, by a veil of deceit and self-deceit. Marx and the whole materialistic movement of which he formed part, had turned the world right way up before their eyes, revealing to them the true springs of human behaviour.

Marxism offered them also a future, bearing unbounded promise to humanity. It predicted that historic necessity would destroy an antiquated form of society and replace it by a new one, in which the existing miseries and injustices would be eliminated. Though this prospect was put forward as a purely scientific observation, it endowed those who accepted it with a feeling of overwhelming moral superiority. They acquired a sense of righteousness, which in a paradoxical manner was fiercely intensified by the mechanical framework in which it was set. Their nihilism had prevented them from demanding justice in the name of justice, or humanity in the name of humanity; these words were banned from their vocabulary and their minds closed to these concepts. But, silenced and repressed, their moral aspirations found an outlet in the scientific prediction of a perfect society. Here was set out a scientific Utopia relying for its fulfilment only on violence. Nihilists could accept, and would eagerly embrace, such a prophecy, which required from its disciples no other belief than that in the force of bodily appetites and yet at the same time satisfied their most extravagant moral hopes. Their sense of righteousness was thus reinforced by a calculated brutality, born of scientific self-assurance. There emerged the modern fanatic, armoured with impenetrable scepticism.

The power of Marxism over the mind is based here on a process exactly inverse of Freudian sublimation. The moral needs of man, which are denied expression in terms of human ideals, are injected into a system of naked power, to which they impart the force of a blind moral passion. With some qualification the same is true of the appeal of National Socialism to the mind of German youth. By offering them an interpretation of history in the materialistic terms of international class-war, Hitler mobilized their sense of civic obligation which would not respond to humane ideals. It was a mistake to regard the Nazi as an untaught savage. His bestiality was carefully groomed by speculations closely reflecting Marxian influence. His contempt for humanitarian ideals had a century of philosophic schooling behind it. The Nazi disbelieves in public morality in the way we disbelieve in witchcraft. It is not that he has never heard of it, but that he thinks he has valid grounds to assert that such a thing cannot exist. If you tell him the contrary, he will think you peculiarly old-fashioned, or simply dishonest.

In such men, the traditional forms for holding moral ideals had been shattered and their moral passions diverted into the only channels which a strictly mechanistic conception of man and society left open to them. We may describe this as a process of *moral inversion*. The morally inverted person has not merely performed a philosophic substitution of moral aims by material purposes, but is acting with the whole force of his homeless moral passions within a purely materialistic framework of purposes.

There remains for me to describe the actual battlefield on which the conflict that led to the downfall of liberty in Europe was fought out. Let me approach the scene from the West. Towards the close of the Four Years' War, we hear from across the Atlantic the voice of Wilson appealing for a new Europe in terms of pure eighteenth-century ideas. "What we seek," he summed up in his declaration of the 4th

July, 1918, "is the reign of law, based upon the consent of the governed and sustained by the organized opinion of mankind." When a few months later Wilson landed in Europe, a tide of boundless hope swept through its lands. They were the old hopes of the eighteenth and nineteenth centuries, only much brighter than ever before.

Wilson's appeal and the response it evoked marked the high tide of the original moral aspirations of Enlightenment. It showed how, in spite of the philosophic difficulties which impaired the foundations of overt moral assertions, such assertions could in practice still be made as vigorously as ever in the regions of Anglo-American influence.

But the great hopes spreading from the Atlantic seaboard were contemptuously rejected by the nihilistic or morally inverted intelligentsia of Central and Eastern Europe. To Lenin, Wilson's language was a huge joke; from Mussolini or Goebbels it might have evoked an angry sneer. And the political theories which these men and their small circle of followers were mooting at the time were soon to defeat the appeal of Wilson and of democratic ideals in general. They were to establish within twenty years or so a comprehensive system of totalitarian governments over Europe, with a good prospect of subjecting the whole world to such government.

The sweeping success of Wilson's opponents was due to the greater appeal which their ideas made on a considerable section of the Central and Eastern nations. Admittedly, their final rise to power was achieved by violence, but not before they had gained sufficient support in every stratum of the population so that they could use violence effectively. Wilson's doctrines were first defeated by the superior convincing power of opposing philosophies, and it is this new and fiercer Enlightenment that has continued ever since to strike relentlessly at every humane and rational principle rooted in the soil of Europe.

The downfall of liberty which followed the success of these attacks everywhere demonstrates in hard facts what I had said before: that freedom of thought is rendered pointless and must disappear, where reason and morality are deprived of their status as a force in their own right. When the judge in court can no longer appeal to law and justice; when neither a witness, nor the newspapers, nor even a scientist reporting on his experiments, can speak the truth as he knows it; when in public life there is no moral principle commanding respect; when the revelations of religion and of art are denied any substance; then there are no grounds left on which any individual may justly make a stand against the rulers of the day. Such is the simple logic of totalitarianism. A nihilistic regime will have to undertake the day-to-day direction of all activities which are otherwise guided by the intellectual and moral principles that nihilism declares empty and void. Principles must be replaced by the decrees of an all-embracing Party Line.

This is why modern totalitarianism, based on a purely materialistic conception of man, is of necessity more oppressive than an authoritarianism enforcing a spiritual creed, however rigid. Take the medieval church even at its worst. The authority of certain texts which it imposed remained fixed over long periods of time and their interpretation was laid down in systems of theology and philosophy, gradually developing over more than a millennium from St. Paul to Aquinas. A good Catholic was not required to change his convictions and reverse his beliefs at frequent intervals, in deference to the secret decisions of a handful of high officials. Moreover, since the authority of the Church was spiritual, it recognized other independent principles outside its own. Though it imposed numerous regulations on individual conduct, there were many parts of life left untouched and governed by other authorities—rivals of the Church— like kings, noblemen, guilds, corporations. And the power of all these was transcended by the growing force of law; while a good deal of speculative and artistic initiative was allowed to pulsate freely through this many-sided system.

The unprecedented oppressiveness of modern totalitarianism has become widely recognized on the Continent to-day and has gone some way towards allaying the feud between the fighters of liberty and the upholders of religion, which had been going on there since the first spread of Enlightenment. Anti-clericalism is not dead, but many who recognize the transcendent obligations and are resolved to preserve a society built on the belief that such obligations are real, have now discovered that they stand much closer to believers in the Bible and in the Christian revelation, than to the nihilist regimes, based on radical disbelief. History will perhaps record the Italian elections of April 1946 as the turning-point. The defeat inflicted there on the Communists by a large Catholic majority was hailed with immense relief by defenders of liberty throughout the world; by many who had been brought up under Voltaire's motto, "Écrasez l'infame!" and had in earlier days voiced all their hopes in that battle-cry.

It would seem to me that on the day when the modern sceptic first placed his trust in the Catholic Church to rescue his liberties against the Frankenstein monster of his own creation, a vast cycle of human thought had come full swing. The sphere of doubt had been circumnavigated. The critical enterprise which gave rise to the Renaissance and the Reformation, and started the rise of our science, philosophy, and art, had matured to its conclusion and had reached its final limits. We have thus begun to live in a new intellectual period, which I would call the post-critical age of Western civilization. Liberalism to-day is becoming conscious of its own fiduciary foundations and is forming an alliance with other beliefs, kindred to its own.

134

The instability of modern liberalism stands in curious contrast to the peacefully continued existence of intellectual freedom through a thousand years of antiquity. Why did the contradiction between liberty and scepticism never plunge the ancient world into a totalitarian revolution, like that of the twentieth century?

We may answer that at least once such a crisis did develop when a number of brilliant young men, whom Socrates had introduced to the pursuit of unfettered inquiry blossomed out as leaders of the Thirty Tyrants. Men like Charmides and Kritias were nihilists, consciously adopting a political philosophy of smash-and-grab which they derived from their Socratic education; and as a reaction to this Socrates was impeached and executed.

Yet I think that these conflicts were never so fierce and far-reaching as the revolutions of the twentieth century. There was an element of passion lacking in antiquity: the prophetic passion of Christian Messianism. The ever-unquenched hunger and thirst after righteousness which our civilization carries in its blood as a heritage of Christianity, does not allow us to settle down in the Stoic manner of antiquity. Modern thought is a mixture of Christian beliefs and Greek doubts. Christian beliefs and Greek doubts are logically incompatible and the conflict between the two has kept Western thought alive and creative beyond precedent. But this mixture is an unstable foundation. Modern totalitarianism is a consummation of the conflict between religion and scepticism. It solves the conflict by embodying our heritage of moral passions in a framework of modern materialistic purposes. The conditions for such an outcome were not present in the age of antiquity, before Christianity had set alight new vast moral hopes in the heart of mankind.

8

The Span of Central Direction[1]

his essay may be labouring the obvious. But obvious though my result may seem, I can find it stated nowhere, while a great deal has been written which contradicts it by implication.

I affirm that the central planning of production—in the rigorous and historically not unwarranted sense of the term—is strictly impossible; the reason being that the number of relations requiring adjustment per unit of time for the functioning of an economic system of n productive units is n-times greater than can be adjusted by subordinating the units to a central authority. Thus, if we insisted in placing the 100,000 business units of a major industrial country under a single technocratic control, replacing all market operations by central allocations of materials to each plant, the rate of economic adjustments would be reduced to about 1 : 100,000 of its usual value and the rate of production would be reduced to the same extent.

The actual figure and even the precise form of the mathematical relationship is unimportant. My point is that

1. *The Manchester School,* 1948.

it can be demonstrated that an overwhelming reduction, amounting to a standstill in the possible rate of production, must arise from the administrative limitations of a system of central direction.

If this is true—and I think it is only too obviously true—then a number of problems arise. If planning is impossible to the point of absurdity, what are the so-called planned economies doing? What about wartime planning? And how can central economic planning, if it is utterly incapable of achievement, be a danger to liberty as it is widely assumed to be?

I shall not face these questions here directly, but I think that the subsequent argument goes a considerable way towards answering them. While I shall emphasize here throughout that the operations of a system of spontaneous order in society, such as the competitive order of a market, cannot be replaced by the establishment of a deliberate ordering agency, this must not be taken as an attempt to overlook or excuse the shortcomings of such automatic systems. It merely implies that, in general, we must either put up with these deficiencies or forgo the operations of the system altogether. For though we may sometimes be able to invent and enforce some new forms of mutual adjustment which will fulfil our purpose better, there is no reason to assume that this will as a rule be possible. This is extensively discussed in a subsequent essay (p. 189).

CORPORATE ORDER

There are many ways of placing human beings into the specifically prescribed positions of a pattern. You may line up people in a row according to size, or assign to each of them a particular seat in a train. But I wish to concentrate here on such forms of specific direction as co-ordinate the full-time activities of a group of people over an extensive period, directing them to the execution of a complex and flexible task and requiring at frequent intervals the re-assignment of the part played by each. Such specific direction must involve the placing of the persons in question under the authority of one superior, with responsibility continuously to re-direct their joint activities. These persons must be organized into a corporation under the authority of a chief executive.

The shape of such corporations is predominantly determined by the fact that the number of subordinates placed directly under the orders of any superior must not exceed his span of control. In the administration of a delicate and rapidly changing task the span of control will usually not exceed 3 to 5. The limit is imposed by the fact that the number of significant relations between subordinates requiring readjustment goes up steeply with the number of subordinates, so that the number of these relations—or more precisely, the rate at which they have to be readjusted—soon outruns the controlling powers of one man's mind.

Since the chief can give orders directly to no more than three to five subordinates, any larger body must be co-ordinated through devolution to successive tiers of subordinate officials. These tiers will broaden out at each stage down to the lowest level, which will contain the men and women actually handling the job. The directions of the chief executive descend to the lowest level through a pyramid of authority, which is also an organ for reporting upwards the events which occur among the workers (or soldiers, etc.) at the base.

In a hierarchic order of this kind, each person's primary task is assigned to him by direction from above and his principal communications regarding the progress of his work take the form of reports to his superior. An official's direct contacts are thus limited to the one man above him and to the few immediate subordinates below him, and any direct official contacts he would make beyond these would short-circuit some of the lines of authority on which the organization relies. If at any point such a contact should exercise a decisive effect on the actions of any member of the organization, it would sever the line of authority connecting him with the centre.

The actions of a perfectly co-ordinated corporate body of this kind (engaged for example in waging a military campaign or conducting a commercial enterprise) are essentially those of the one man at the top. The chief alone is allowed to deal with the wider perspectives and the longer-range problems of the corporation; he alone can evolve a strategy and exercise powers of judgment of a higher order. All others have only fragmentary tasks to perform within the limits of the changing directives issued to them by their immediate superiors.

A corporation thus elaborates the ideas of the chief executive and his advisers into a wealth of detail, co-ordinating the men at the bottom of the pyramid who carry them out, and assigning and continuously re-assigning to each a specific function. The actions carried out at the base of the pyramid may therefore be said to be *centrally directed* or *centrally planned*.

The essential limitations of this method can be readily recognized from the previous description. The task assigned to a centrally directed corporation must possess natural unity, in order that it may be successfully handled by one man at the top; it must be capable of subdivision in a series of successive stages, each resultant part once more forming a natural unit which can be assigned to one man as his particular job; and the co-ordination of these parts must be amenable to control by one person.

Tasks which have a profound natural unity very often cannot be subdivided at all. Poetry and painting, invention and discovery, are essentially one-man jobs. Other tasks, though they can be broken down to subsidiary jobs, will often not be suited for repeated subdivision into a large number of successive stages. Hence corporate organizations will as a rule not grow to large sizes so long as they are performing closely co-ordinated, complex and flexible operations. Where we meet large hierarchic organizations which can apparently be extended indefinitely, like railways or post offices, they turn out to be rather loose aggregates performing standardized functions. Armies may appear as exceptions, for they are flexible and yet maintain a measure of organic unity, while comprising millions of members. But the co-ordination of fighting units within a campaigning army is really quite loose; though this may go unnoticed since an army's task consists merely in defeating another army, which is organized in a similarly clumsy manner.

The productive process of a modern industrial system involves the allocation to each plant of materials produced by other plants and the daily readjustments of these allocations of materials, in response to the variations in their supply and the changes of demand from other plants and from consumers. This system of allocations represents a coherent task of great complexity, which continuously requires readjustment at every plant. If this task had to be directed centrally, it would have to be carried out through a single corporate body, with the plants at its base. Such a corporate body, however, would not satisfy the conditions outlined in the foregoing paragraphs and hence could not function. The purpose of this paper is to demonstrate this thesis, by attempting an approximately quantitative comparison of the administrative *powers* of a corporate body with the size of the administrative *task*, involved in the conduct of a modern industrial system of production.

THE SPAN OF CENTRAL DIRECTION

SPONTANEOUS ORDER COMPARED WITH CORPORATE ORDER

Consider the possibilities of spontaneous order in society. There are a number of cases of this type which do not interest us here. For instance, passengers will distribute themselves over the compartments of a train by mutual adjustment in an orderly fashion, first filling all window seats facing the engine, then all other window seats and the corridor corner seats, etc., until all seats are filled, with passengers occupying the various grades of places in a descending sequence of advantage in accordance with the sequence of their arrival on the platform. We shall not deal here with such occasional and inessential forms of mutual adjustment, but turn our attention to spontaneously ordered systems in which persons mutually adjust their full-time activities over a prolonged period, resulting in a complex and yet highly adaptable co-ordination of these actions.

I have said earlier on in a preliminary fashion that the two kinds of order—the deliberate and the spontaneous—are mutually exclusive. I must now qualify this statement. The establishment of a corporate body does not exclude all mutual adjustments between its members. In a battle-line, neighbouring units belonging to different divisions will mutually assist each other without awaiting instructions from army command. Intelligent regard for what the next man is doing is indispensable to the successful operation of any corporate authority. Such mutual adjustment, however, must never go beyond a certain limit. It should *condition* the actions of subordinates, but must never *determine* them. Only if the superior remains decisive in determining the actions of his subordinates, can he remain responsible for the co-ordination of their activities. If persons operating at the base of a pyramid of authority (or at any other level of it) were to allow their actions to be primarily determined by direct mutual contacts, the authority above them would be nullified. In this sense it is true that the two kinds of order are mutually exclusive.

I shall show next that the span of control (i.e. the number of adjustable relations) is much larger within a system of mutual adjustment than under the authority of a corporate body, and that the task of administering a process of industrial production requires the readjustment of a number of relations far exceeding the span of control of a corporate body; and that consequently, (1) a corporate body cannot even remotely cope with such a task and (2) this can be carried out only under a system of mutual adjustment, so far as it can be rationally administered at all. This argument requires a comparative estimate of the spans of control of corporate bodies on the one hand and spontaneous systems on the other.

Consider two small teams, say of five persons each, representing respectively examples of our two kinds of order. Let one team be the five forwards in a game of football, charging at the opposite goal and co-ordinating themselves by mutual adjustment. Let the other team be the crew of a small craft riding a heavy sea, where each man's actions are co-ordinated to the others' by the captain's commands. This gives us for comparison two cases, one of spontaneous and the other of corporate order, each covering a network of relationships in a system of five units. We may take it that this network comprises the same number of independently adjustable relationships in both cases.

Call f the number of adjustments which each football forward can effectively make per minute in response to the action of the other four players, and call c the number of orders the captain can effectively issue per minute to his crew. If the number of relations adjusted per football player per minute is measured by f, then the corresponding number for the crew of five sailors is $c/5$. Now self-adjustment is swifter than the adjustment of others by issuing orders to them, so f is larger than c and it is, of course, five times larger still than $c/5$. The number of relations adjusted per person per minute is therefore greater in the self-co-ordinated than in the authoritatively controlled team. But this does not bring out the decisive difference between the two types, which becomes apparent only in systems of larger size.

Let us examine an extension of the numbers involved in either type and compare the corresponding increase in the number of relationships brought under control. A system of spontaneous order is entirely on one level and all additional units accrue to it on the same level. A corporate system, on the other hand, can be extended to any considerable extent only by increasing the height of the pyramid through the addition of new tiers. In a corporate body, in which the span of control of each superior is 5 and this span is fully utilized throughout, each lower level will contain five times more persons than the level above it, and if the number of levels is l, the total number p of persons comprised will be:

$$p = 1 + 5 + 5^2 + 5^3 + \ldots + 5^{l-1}$$

A sea captain in a storm, issuing orders directly to each of his crew of five, would be at the very limit of his span of control, and we may take it, therefore, that the number c of orders given by him per minute would represent the maximum that can be effectively issued by any superior to his subordinates. The number per minute of relations adjustable per person at the base of the pyramid will hence be represented for the corporate order by c-times the number $p - 5^{l-1}$ of superior officers issuing orders to subordinates, divided by the number 5^{l-1} of persons at the base of the pyramid. Carrying out the calculation, this number will be found to be only slightly greater than $c/5$, that is, of the same order as for the captain and his crew of five. In other words: an increase in the size of a corporate body leaves the number of relations *per capita* which can be adjusted between the persons whose actions it ultimately governs, practically unaffected.

Take now the extension of a system of spontaneous order. We shall again assume that the performance of the individual participants remains unchanged while the system is extended; which means in this case that the same rate of self-adjustment f that applied to the chain of football forwards is assumed throughout. But we must now consider the fact that f was a proper measure of the rate of adjustment of *relations* between five football forwards, in comparing them with a crew of five sailors, only because the two groups are equinumerous. For there is no reason why in general the member of a team adjusting his actions to that of his fellows should not take into account and adjust himself to the actions of more than four of his fellows. Football forwards will actually do this quite often and there are many systems of spontaneous order for which the number of relations affected by each act of self-adjustment is much greater still.

Think, for example, of the consumers of gas at a time when there is a shortage resulting in abnormally low gas-pressure. A number of people will be unable to heat their bath-water to an acceptable temperature and will rather not have a bath. Every person deciding in view of the existing gas-pressure for or against having a bath will directly affect the decision of all other consumers, making up their minds on the same question about the same time. We have here a system of mutual adjustments, each of which affects thousands of relations. This number may become much greater still when a system of mutual adjustment is based on organized publicity. This is realized, most notably, in a public market where millions of consumers draw on the same supplies. Each consumer adjusts his purchases to the ruling price, which he affects in his turn by his purchases.

The allocation of raw materials through the market to the plants constituting a productive system, and the suitable readjustment of this allocation in view of the changing supplies of raw materials and the varying demands of consumers—with which we are principally concerned here—is clearly another instance of a large self-co-ordinating system in which each decision of one unit re-adjusts its relations to a great number of other units.

In these large spontaneously ordered systems, the number of relations readjusted by each self-adjustment may be many thousand times greater than in a system of five football forwards. Assuming the (maximum) rate of self-adjustment still to be f, the rate of adjustment of relations per person may thus become many thousand times f.

We recognize here the immense quantitative superiority of a system of spontaneous order. When such a system is extended in size, there may result an almost indefinite increase in the rate at which relations are readjusted per member. This is in sharp contrast to the conditions prevailing within a corporate system, the growth of which does not materially enhance the number of relations per person that can be re-adjusted per unit of time. In other words, the span of control of a spontaneous system, divided by the number of its members, increases proportionately to this number, while the span of control of a corporate system, divided by the number of its ultimate subordinates, is practically unaffected by an increase in the size of the system. Or alternatively: the span of control of the former type of system may be said to increase with the square of its size, while that of the latter goes only proportionately to size.

An authority charged with replacing by deliberate direction the functions of a large self-adjusting system, would be placed in the position of a man charged with controlling single-handed a machine requiring for its operation the simultaneous working of thousands of levers. Its legal powers would avail it nothing. By insisting on them, it could only paralyse a system which it failed to govern.

I have avoided so far any reference to the absolute number of adjustable relations within a group, for this is a very uncertain magnitude. But the use of comparative numbers, which I have adopted instead, has brought with it an undesirable degree of abstraction. It may be worth while, therefore, to reformulate the argument in more concrete terms, even at the risk of some drastic over-simplification.

Look at the organizational chart of a corporate authority, reduced to its bare bones. For simplicity's sake let us take the span of control to be 3 throughout the pyramid of authority. In Fig. 1 I have drawn the chart for a pyramid of four levels. There is the chief at the top and 27 ultimate subordinates at the base; there are two tiers of intermediate superiors between them. The chart is set out in space to show the relations controlled at each level by the superiors at the higher level. Each particular relation is indicated by a dotted line, connecting the units which it relates. The total number r of these relations is seen to be:

$$r = 3 + 3^2 + 3^3$$

and in general: $r = 3 + 3^2 + \ldots + 3^{l-1}$, where l is the total number of levels. At the same time, the number m of ulti-

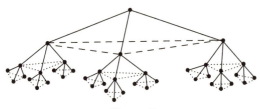

Figure 1

mate subordinates at the base of the pyramid is 3^{l-1}, so that the ratio $i = r/m$, which measures the number of relations per person governed by the corporate body, comes out as:

$$i = 3^{2-l} + 3^{3-l} + \ldots + 3^{l-1}$$
$$= (^1/_3)^{l-2} + (^1/_3)^{l-3} + \ldots + 1.$$

Thus for $l = 2$ the complexity of relatedness i has its minimum value 1 and this value increases with an increasing number of levels asymptotically to 3/2. Had we assumed a larger span of control—which would be closer to the truth —the increase would be even less. It is always negligible. The same holds, of course, for the number of relations adjusted per person per unit of time, if we assume (as before) that the rate at which superiors issue their instructions remains constant as the height of the pyramid is increased by the addition of new levels.

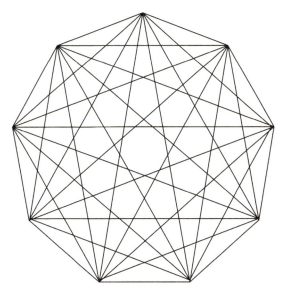

Figure 2

For comparison, we now turn to a system of spontaneous order; instead of the 9 ultimate subordinates, we shall consider 9 members of such a system. We may imagine them arranged in a circle as in Fig. 2, with connecting lines indicating the relation of each to the others. From each member there issue eight lines, or in general m-1 lines, if m is the number of members of the self-adjusting system. Thus the complexity of relatedness, and with it the rate of readjustment of relations per person—instead of remaining practically unchanged as in the case of an increase in the size of a corporate body—is seen to mount up proportionately to the membership of a system of spontaneous order. We arrive here at the same result as before.

The fact that for large systems, the administrative span of control exercised by spontaneous mutual adjustment becomes overwhelmingly greater than that of a corporate body of corresponding size, seems to me so important and yet—in spite of its massiveness—in a way so elusive, that I shall give yet a third variant of its demonstration, this time avoiding all algebra.

Take a group of three ultimate subordinates under one superior at the base of the pyramid in Fig. 1. Any one of these will have relations of the same complexity in respect to any other member of the group, as if the group formed a self-adjusting system. (The rate of readjustment of relations per member will be less, for adjustment by a superior is slower than self-adjustment—but we need not consider this here.) Examine now the relations of any member of *one group* to a member of any *other group* of ultimate subordinates. We can see that these relations are of two kinds. There is one kind of relationship between the members of different groups, having a common superior at a level just above that of their direct superior. This relationship may be compared to that between first cousins. Each ultimate subordinate in Fig. 1 has six administrative first cousins. There is a second kind of relationship between ultimate subordinates in Fig. 1, which makes them administrative second cousins, as their common superior is placed one level higher than that of first cousins; in Fig. 1 each ultimate subordinate has 18 second cousins.

Consider more closely the relations between first cousins. Their common superior receives reports about the situation and achievements of the different groups to which the first cousins belong, and issues orders to the official in charge of these different groups. This process co-ordinates the activities of the groups as wholes and will in general affect all the members of one group jointly in their relation to all the members of another group. Take, for example, as groups of ultimate subordinates the crews of several small craft under the command of their captains and suppose that the ships form a fleet under the command of one senior officer. Orders issued by the officer will affect the relations between all sailors in a pair of different vessels in a similar manner. They will not adjust—as the captains of each craft do—any specific individual relation between members of the same crew. As a result, no individual relations of any kind will be established between members of different crews. This is generally true for all relations between administrative cousins and becomes increasingly marked for second and third cousins, etc. These are adjusted to one another *in blocks of increasing sizes* and the adjustment between the members of such blocks is wholesale and undifferentiated.

This shows once more the comparatively small span of control exercised by corporate authority and that if any attempt were made to replace a spontaneous system by a corporate order, it would result in cutting down to a tiny fraction the operations of any large system of that kind.

One would hardly expect to find under these circumstances any serious suggestion of replacing the functions of a major self-adjusting system by the directions of a central authority. Yet contemporary thought is pervaded by the fallacy of central planning, particularly as regards industrial production. The belief prevails widely that direct physical controls, consciously applied from one centre, can in general fully replace adjustments spreading automatically through a network of market relations. It underlies the Socialist movement and is even shared, in more attenuated forms, by most of those who oppose Socialism. The rigorous free-traders, for example, who urgently warn against the danger of enslavement by economic planning, thereby imply (often without intending it) that economic planning is feasible, though at the price of liberty. Indeed, a great deal of public discussion on Socialist policy in Britain appears to be based to-day on the supposition, that a fully directed economic system could be established by adopting the necessary totalitarian measures.

The studies by professional economists to the feasibility of central economic planning have pursued a tortuous course. Before the Russian Revolution the question had not been examined systematically, but as early as 1920 Professor Ludwig v. Mises started a critique of Socialism on the grounds that in the absence of a market for factors of production these could not be rationally allocated to industrial plants and that, in consequence, a centrally directed economy could not function. His book, *Die Gemeinwirtschaft,* first published in 1922 (and later, in a revised English translation, under the title *Socialism,* in 1936), elaborated this criticism in detail. The subsequent developments of the discussion were, I believe, again largely determined by events in

150

Russia. At the time of L. v. Mises' first writing, the meanings of Socialism and central economic planning were (as I shall show later in this paper) unquestioningly identified with the elimination of the market as a means of allocating resources and its replacement by a system of direct central allocations. The attempt made in Russia during the period extending from 1919 to March 1921, to establish such a system broke down in chaos as v. Mises had rightly predicted; nor did the subsequent retreat to capitalism under the N.E.P. during 1921–1928 bring any evidence to contradict his thesis. But once the Five-Year Plans got under way the situation seemed to have radically altered. This certainly was Socialism in the sense of State ownership and it also seemed to be a centrally directed economy. Yet it undoubtedly was a functioning economy; whatever its failings, the system could not be said to be utterly devoid of rationality.

It seems to me that in response to this new phase in Russia, both the opponents and adherents of Socialism somewhat changed their grounds. An eminent critic of Socialism, Professor F. H. Knight, joined issue with v. Mises by pointing out that economic theory did not contradict the possibility of a centrally directed economy.[1] It only required that such an economy should be administered according to marginal principles.

The position reached by Knight on these grounds is important and shall be illustrated here by a few quotations from the paper just mentioned. Knight uses the term "collectivism" (p. 258) to designate what I call a centrally directed economy. Of this he says: ". . . there is no difficulty in imagining, that the constitution and laws of a society might be changed from, say, the form which they have in the

1. The Place of Marginal Economics in a Collective System, *American Economic Review*, 1936, Supplement, p. 259.

United States at this moment to the form of a thorough-going collectivism and that most of the individuals in the country should continue to do substantially the same things and to enjoy the same fruits of their activity as before" (p. 258). The proviso is made that the State power should have "an ideally honest and competent administrative system" at its service. "There are several fundamental respects" —it is added—"in which the economy of a collectivist system would be enormously simplified in comparison with private property." The trade cycle would be eliminated, the problem of taxation ideally solved, the harms of monopoly avoided (p. 263). Yet the collectivist system is rejected by Knight on the grounds that it would give the government "absolute power over the lives of its citizens."[2]

Knight seems to conclude here (perhaps from Stalin's Five-Year Plans) that centrally directed economy can be worked by a totalitarian political system. Similar views, disseminated particularly through v. Hayek's *The Road to Serfdom* (1944), have become widely accepted. Professor v. Mises himself seems to move towards them in his recent writings when asserting that a planned economy involves totalitarianism.[3] They seem to permeate much of J. Jewkes's

2. In a later paper published in *Ethics* (1940) and reprinted in his book *Freedom and Reform*, pp. 129–162, Professor Knight discusses Socialism on the basis of the proposals for a publicly owned marketing economy, in the sense of Oscar Lange, A. P. Lerner and others. Since such proposals involve in my view the abandonment of a centrally directed economy, their critique by Professor Knight does not refer to the problem with which I am concerned here.

3. "Men must choose between the market economy and socialism. The State can preserve the market economy in protecting life, health and private property against violent and fraudulent aggression; or it can itself control the conduct of all production activities. If it is not the consumers by means of demand and supply on the market, it must be the government by compulsion." L. von Mises, *Planned Chaos* (1947), p. 34.

critique of the British Socialist experiment in his *Ordeal by Planning* (1948).

The new Socialist school of thought which rapidly gained vigour from 1933 onwards may be regarded as another response to the Five-Year Plans. Its representatives, H. D. Dickinson,[4] Oscar Lange,[5] A. P. Lerner,[6] J. E. Meade[7] and E. F. M. Durbin,[8] opposed the argument of v. Mises on the grounds that public ownership did not exclude the use of the market for allocating resources between enterprises. They propose the combination of the two as a solution to the difficulties pointed out by v. Mises.

The outcome of this line of thought was most peculiar. Unnoticed both by its advocates and its critics, modern Socialist theory, by adopting the principles of commerce, has quietly abandoned the cardinal claim of Socialism: the central direction of industrial production. Apart from calling his chief economic authority by the name of Central Planning Board, Oscar Lange (1938) makes no reference to planning in the proper sense. Mr. Dickinson (1938) opens his book with a declaration favouring resolute centralized planning; but by the time he developed his scheme the result is this:

> In one or two matters, perhaps, considerations of social policy would be planned on their merits. . . . The great majority of lines of production would be carried on automatically within the given framework of costs and prices so as to supply goods to consumers according to their preference as indicated by the market. (p. 222)

4. *Economic Journal,* June 1933; *Economics of Socialism,* 1938.

5. *Economic Journal,* Oct. 1936; *The Economic Theory of Socialism,* 1938.

6. *Review of Economic Studies,* Oct. 1934.

7. *Economic Analysis and Policy,* 1936.

8. *Economic Journal,* Dec. 1936.

From the original Socialist point of view, Mr. M. Dobb's lonely protest against this school of thought appears thoroughly justified. "Either planning means overriding the autonomy of separate decisions [he writes] or apparently it means nothing at all."[9] And he proceeds to pour ridicule on the whole scheme: "That in a socialist economy it should be thought necessary for managers of various plants, having ascertained the various data about productivity, to play an elaborate game of bidding for capital on the market, instead of transmitting the information direct to some planning authority, is a 'Heath Robinson' kind of suggestion which it is hard to take seriously. Moreover, it has the positive disadvantage that in playing such a game the managers of socialist enterprises would be as much 'in blinkers' as to the concurrent decisions made elsewhere, as are private *entrepreneurs* to-day, and thus would be subject to a similar degree of competitive uncertainty."[10]

To me it seems that these varied, shifting and obscure ideas concerning economic planning, all reflect the same essential deficiency. They lack throughout the clear recognition of the fact that a centrally directed industrial system is administratively impossible—impossible in the same sense in which it is impossible for a cat to swim the Atlantic.

Rarely does one find this pointed out. Leo Trotsky is one who placed it on record. In 1918–1920 he had been himself the protagonist of a rigorously centralized system. But later, chastened no doubt by its disastrous results, he declared that it would require a Universal Mind as conceived by Laplace to make a success of such a system.[11] Professor

9. M. Dobb, *Political Economy and Capitalism* (revised edition, 1940), p. 275.

10. Ibid, p. 305.

11. Trotsky, *Soviet Economy in Danger* (1931).

A. P. Lerner,[12] quoting Trotsky with vigorous approval, adds that any attempt to realize the central direction of economic life must inevitably collapse in administrative chaos. I have also found one reasoned statement of this view. Mr. J. E. Meade has given it as early as 1935[13] in the following passage, discussing the scope of a Planning Commission charged with allocating productive resources to the exclusion of their distribution through the market:

> No amount of consultation with engineers and technicians will enable the commission to make sure whether by shifting a little of this raw material from A to B and a little of this land from B to C, a little of this grade of labour from C to A and of this machinery from C to E and a little of this raw material from D to E and some of this land from E to A it is possible to increase the output of A without changing the output of any other product.

This expresses it clearly that the impossibility of central economic direction lies in the much shorter span of control of a corporate body as compared with a self-adjusted system. My task has been to demonstrate this disparity in semi-quantitative terms.

AN EXPERIMENT IN CENTRAL PLANNING

It may be inevitable that with our growing sophistication speculative excesses should increasingly determine the course of history; it is also perhaps pardonable that great hopes thus misplaced should incent men to riot, cruelty and destruction; but it is surely insufferable that lessons gained at such sacrifice should be allowed wilfully to be obscured and thrust into oblivion. The attempt to establish a centrally directed economy

12. A. P. Lerner, *Economics of Control* (1944), pp. 62, 98, 119.

13. J. E. Meade, *Economic Analysis and Policy* (1935), p. 199.

during the early years of the Russian Revolution—which was paid for by the death of over five million people—must not be allowed to be erased from history. It should be retained as a decisive experience of mankind.

The experiment of Central Planning in Russia was introduced gradually in 1919, increasingly sharpened throughout 1920 and then terminated—to avoid further disaster—in March, 1921. During some of that period, civil war was still in progress in parts of the country and the Soviet Government has ever since tried to conceal the catastrophic failure of central planning, by falsely attributing the need for the economic policy of the time and its devastating results to the exigencies of war. Hence the official description of that phase "War Communism."

Yet contemporary evidence is clear and conclusive. I shall give just a few brief illustrations of it. A typical statement which I shall reproduce here in the enthusiastic italics of the author, is a passage from a pamphlet by W. P. Miljutin,[14] dated 29th June, 1920, and published by the Communist International in 1921. "All enterprises," he writes, "and all branches of industry *are considered as one enterprise. . . . The unity of the centralized economy, which is organized according to plan by the authorities of the Soviet Union . . . that is the economic organization of the Soviet power.*" According to this report, centralization was in fact very far-reaching. Each plant reported directly, or indirectly, to the Supreme Economic Council and received its production programme allotted to it from there. Plants directly controlled by the Supreme Economic Council received their raw material assigned to them directly by the Council, while locally ad-

14. W. P. Miljutin, *Die Organisation der Volkswirtschaft in Sowjet Russland,* Verlag der Kommunistischen Internationale. Auslieferungsstelle für Deutschland: Verlagsbuchhandlung Carl Heym Nachf., Hamburg. The book is dated by the author: 29th June, 1920.

ministered plants were supplied by the local board in question. All plants received their business capital from the centre and were provided with rations for their workers by the Food Commissariat, acting in conjunction with the Supreme Economic Council. All products, including those of the territorially administered industries, were to be delivered to the Supreme Economic Council and centrally distributed through its "Utilization Department." Products used for production purposes were allotted to the respective industries, while finished industrial products were distributed to consumers through a section working in conjunction with the Commissariat for Food.

Foodstuffs and agricultural raw materials were obtained by requisitioning and to a smaller part from Soviet estates. Following on the nationalization of the banks on 14th December, 1917,[15] the use of money was discouraged, neglected and discredited in every way. The following statement made in 1918 by the Commissariat for Finance is typical of the reference to money in the Communist literature of the period:

> When the main part of our socialist programme is carried out, money will become superfluous as an instrument of exchange and distribution; and will be abolished ... with the passing of power to the proletariat, economy as regards the state purse is quite unnecessary. ... Strict calculation, economy in spending and conformity of revenue to expenditure are not essential.[16]

The major part of all wages was paid in kind (pajki), this process having become the main channel for distributing goods to the consumers. L. Kritzmann, writing in August,

15. Boris Brutzkus, *Economic Planning in Soviet Russia* (1935), p. 100.

16. Quoted by L. Lawton, *An Economic History of Soviet Russia,* p. 100. See also reference to Eighth Congress of the Soviets, ibid, p. 108.

1920,[17] describes this system and concludes that: "Legal trade has almost completely ceased to exist; it is replaced by the distributive organs of the State."

The consequences of this policy showed themselves in a complete breakdown of the productive apparatus. The major industries of the country—which had been entirely brought under governmental control—came virtually to a standstill. The towns, unable to feed themselves by offering industrial goods to the farmers, were ravaged by famine. Large parts of their population drifted into the countryside.[18] The government tried to redress the balance by requisitioning food by force from the still privately managed farmsteads. In the ensuing struggle, the peasants proved the stronger. Peasant risings, followed by strikes in Leningrad factories and a mutiny of the sailors of Kronstadt, finally forced Lenin in March, 1921, to repeal the whole system. By that time, however, the peasants had reduced sowing to less than 50 per cent. of the areas sown in 1913. A famine ensued, which according to recent estimates, cost 5.5 million lives.[19]

Most of the Communist commentators of the time continued to praise, in the very midst of the rapidly spreading catastrophe, the achievements of the new economic system.[20] But by the end of 1920, some of the leaders at any

17. I. Larin and L. Kritzmann, *Wirtschaftsleben und Wirtschaftlicher Aufbau in Sowjet Russland,* 1917–1920. Verlag der Kommunistischen Internationale. Auslieferungsstelle für Deutschland: Verlagsbuchhandlung Carl Heym, Nachf., Hamburg (1921).

18. For a description of these disasters see the *Official History of the Bolshevik Party* (1938).

19. Frank Lorrimer, *The Population of the Soviet Union;* League of Nations, Geneva, 1946.

20. "[The] experiences of the last years have proven that the machinery of the economic dictatorship of the proletariat is functioning securely

rate were having misgivings concerning the task they had embarked upon. Stalin, for one, had certainly ceased to think that the economy of a collective system was particularly simple to run. Speaking on the 7th November, 1920, Stalin complained in the following terms of the special difficulties in building up Communism:

> ... we were building not bourgeois economy where everyone pursues his own private interests and does not worry about the state as a whole, pays no heed to the question of planned, organized economy on a national scale. No, we were building a socialist society. This means that the needs of the society as a whole have to be taken into consideration, that economy has to be organized on all-Russian scale in a planned, conscious manner. No doubt this task is incomparably more complicated and more difficult.[21]

There is on record also a most illuminating speech made by Trotsky in (or about) December 1920, justifying before a national organization of women workers the hardships of the time as due to the inherent difficulties of a centrally directed production. I shall give here only one sentence, ruefully referring to the facile assumptions of central planners:

> All this is easily said, but even in a small farm of 500 desjatines, in which there are various agricultural branches represented, it is necessary to preserve certain proportions; to regulate our vast, far-flung, disorganized economic life so that the various boards should maintain the necessary cross-connections and feed each other, so to speak—for example when it is necessary to build

---

and according to plan. Economic life is being effectively directed and in place of the chaotic, atomized, capitalist economy there is gradually emerging a uniform economic life, built up according to socialist principles."—Miljutin, loc. cit., p. 13.

21. J. Stalin, *The October Revolution*, Martin Lawrence, London. (Printed in the Soviet Union.)

workers' houses, one board should give so many nails as the other gives planks and the third building materials—to achieve such proportionality, such internal correspondence, that is a difficult task which the Soviet power has yet to achieve.[22]

It almost seems as if the first inkling had already reached Trotsky at this time of the need for a Universal Mind to cope with the problem of a centrally directed economy.

The disastrous collapse of the experiment, made in Soviet Russia in the years 1919–1921 for the establishment of a centrally directed economy, is the key to the understanding of the economic policy of Russia in the years that followed. An essential part of that policy was to make the world forget the original aims of Socialism and its abysmal failure at its first trial, while trying to dress up as a planned economy a productive system operating through the market. For this policy it was necessary to misrepresent the planning experiment of the period 1919–1921 as mere emergency legislation, designed to meet the temporary requirements of the blockade and the civil war. Since this version of history has been widely accepted by Western writers, a few more remarks may be added in its refutation.

The measures taken by the government to establish a system of Socialist Planning could, on internal evidence, have nothing to do with the blockade, the civil war or the wars of intervention. For no financial authority would expressly rejoice as the Soviet Government did in the spread of a runaway inflation because it is conducting a war, or is being faced by a blockade. Moreover, none of the decrees or resolutions issued by the Soviet authorities and representative bodies of the Soviet Union for the purpose of establishing a Socialist Planned Economy, do so much as mention the war or the blockade, or give the slightest hint that the

22. *Russische Rundschau* (Moskow), issue of 22nd December, 1920, p. 7.

measures proposed or decreed are meant to be temporary, to be reversed in peace-time. The contrary is true. They are considered as the first stage in the process of achieving even more complete central control of industry. Besides, by the autumn of 1920 all fighting had ceased in and around Soviet Russia. Yet the campaign towards the establishment of planned economy went on until the riots of March 1921 forced its sudden abandonment. In the speech quoted above (made on 7th November, 1920), Stalin, looking back on "the first great difficulties in constructing Socialism" and welcoming the return, at last, to conditions of peace, makes no reference to any proposed change of policy, but suggests on the contrary that further progress on Socialist lines would henceforth be easier in view of the cessation of hostilities. Nor does the speech of Trotsky of December 1920, also dealing with the difficulties of Socialism, give any hint of the alleged connection between war and Socialist planning. The records show in fact quite plainly that the measures taken to establish a centrally planned economy were redoubled in the period following the return of peaceful conditions. This was clearly described by Farbman as follows:[23] " 'The decree for the complete nationalization of all industries, including small-scale enterprise' (that is to say, all undertakings employing more than ten workers, and also all those employing more than five workers if with mechanical power) was issued 'under date 30th November, 1920: the decree that the levying of taxes was to cease, because money no longer functioned as a means of payment, under date 3rd February, 1921. In December 1920 . . . the Eighth Soviet Congress passed the most Utopian of all the resolutions of the days of War Communism, the resolution concerning the socialization of peasant agriculture. Special

23. *After Lenin,* by Michael Farbman (1924), p. 41, quoted by S. and B. Webb, in *Soviet Communism,* (1935), Vol. I, p. 544.

committees were to be appointed to prescribe the scope and the kind of cultivation to be practised on every one of the twenty-five millions of peasant farms.' Peasant farming, said this resolution, 'must be conducted in accordance with a unified plan, under a unified management.'"

The Webbs, though they quote Farbman's evidence proving the contrary, still accept Lenin's explanation given *after* the event, that "military communism" was meant only as "a provisional measure" in response to the necessities of war.[24] This is repeated by M. Dobb in his *Soviet Economic Development since 1917* (1948).[25]

There can actually be no doubt that the economic disaster of 1921 was caused by the administrative chaos ensuing from the attempt of a centrally operated economic system. The contemporary Soviet leaders whom I mentioned, when dealing with the economic hardships of the time, emphasized that these had their origin in the difficulty of building up Socialism. There are utterances on record by leaders like Preobrazensky and Lenin, immediately after the collapse of the attempt at a centrally planned economy, referring to the fact that since the return of peace people had found these hardships unbearable, as they realized that they were not merely temporary effects of war-like conditions. It

24. S. and B. Webb, *Soviet Communism* (1935), Vol. I, p. 544.

25. Mr. Dobb's account of the events does not materially differ from that given in my text, which was completed before his book came out. Yet he rejects as superficial the view that the Soviet government actually tried to establish Communism at that time and met with disaster in consequence. The only *contemporary* evidence adduced by him for this view is an irrelevant remark of Lenin "that the aid of the printing press can only be regarded as a temporary measure." This is followed by the usual quotations from Lenin and other Soviet writers *before* and *after* the event. On such slender grounds does Mr. Dobb give renewed circulation to the fundamental misrepresentation of history fabricated by Lenin and his followers.

is enough to quote on this point the *Official History of the Bolshevik Party*, published in 1938:

> As long as the war lasted [it says] people acquiesced to these deficiencies and hardships; they mostly did not even notice them. But now that the war was over, people suddenly realized that these defects and hardships were unbearable and demanded their immediate termination.

The connection between cause and effect in this matter seems to be conclusively proven by the last phase which brought the experiment to an end and also by the subsequent course of events. We have, firstly, the uprising of peasants and of *workers* and sailors demanding the restoration of trade—"The Soviets without the Communist Party!"[26] Secondly, Lenin's decision in March 1921, immediately following on the quelling of the revolt, to cancel some of the fundamental measures of a centrally directed economy and to permit their replacement by commercial relations, followed by a series of measures restoring one feature of capitalism after another. We have, lastly, an economic recovery of unparalleled steepness, achieved immediately on the abandonment of central economic direction and on the re-establishment of capitalistic commercial relations.

The early phase of the Russian Revolution thus presents an experiment, as clear as history is ever likely to provide, in which (1) Socialist economic planning was pressed home; (2) this had eventually to be abandoned on the grounds that the measures adopted had caused an unparalleled economic disaster, and (3) the abandonment of the Socialist measures and the restoration of capitalist methods of production retrieved economic life from disaster and set it on the road to rapid recovery.

26. S. and B. Webb, *Soviet Communism*, Vol. I, p. 545. (1938).

OTHER EXAMPLES

THE ILLUSION OF CENTRAL PLANNING

But am I not proving too much? Surely the planet to-day is bristling with governments committed to economic planning and filling fat volumes with columns of figures, setting out Four-Year Plans and Five-Year Plans; putting out every now and then hectic reports on the progress made in the execution of these plans. Are these governments not actually doing—and massively achieving in the face of the whole world—precisely that of which I have so rigorously proved the complete infeasibility?[27]

The confrontation does not embarrass my argument. I still maintain that whatever these governments may be actually doing, the sets of figures which they embody in their elaborate economic plans have little bearing on their achievements. Malinowski has pointed out that the attribution of magical powers to chieftains lends them an authority for leadership, which is indispensable to the society under their dominion. The economic plans of to-day probably have as much practical value for the good government of people who believe in them as had the magical formulae of old; but no more.

This follows already from what had been said before, but in view of the great importance of the question, I want to prove my point once more, directly. A few preliminary re-

27. In the short time since this essay was written and first published, this practice has been so rapidly going out of fashion this side of the Iron Curtain, that it seems necessary to recall a few examples of the kind of detailed plans I am referring to. A famous one was the "Monnet Plan" (see *Rapport General sur le Premier Plan de Modernisation et d'Equipment*, Nov. 1946–Jan. 1947, issued by the Presidence du Governement, Commissariat General du Plan du Modernisation et d'Equipment, Paris.) A detailed Four-Years Plan of the Marshall countries was issued in Reports of the Committee of European Co-operation, July–Sept. 1947; Vol. I, General Report; Vol. II, Technical Reports. See also the British *Economic Surveys* 1947 and 1948 (White Papers).

marks may serve to introduce this. Obviously, a system of spontaneous order may have corporate bodies as its members; industrial corporations can be seen mutually adjusted to the use of the same market of resources and selling their goods in the same consumers' market. The operations of each corporate body may be said to proceed according to a plan, and the idea of overall central direction involves, therefore, a fusion of the several plans to one single comprehensive plan. If, as we maintain, the idea of central direction replacing the functions of self-adjusted order is absurd, then the idea of this fusion must also be absurd.

Bearing this in mind, let us now examine the structure of a national production plan. Such plans state the sum of various types of goods and services that are to be produced. The products are divided into classes and sub-classes. We may see for example Industry and Agriculture as our main divisions. Then Industry may be subdivided into Production of Raw Materials, Finished Products and Industrial Services, while Agriculture may again fall into parts, such as Food Production, Forestry and Raw Materials for Industry. Each of these classes can be subdivided again into sub-classes and this process can be continued until we finally come down to the proposed quantities of individual products, which form the ultimate items of the plan.

At first sight, this looks exactly like a true plan, namely like a comprehensive purpose elaborated in detail through successive stages; the kind of plan, in fact, which can be carried out only by appropriate central direction.

But in reality such an alleged plan is but a meaningless summary of an aggregate of plans, dressed up as a single plan. It is as if the manager of a team of chess-players were to find out from each individual player what his next move was going to be and would then sum up the result by saying: "The plan of my team is to advance 45 pawns by one place, move 20 bishops by an average of three places, 15 castles by an average of four places, etc." He could pretend to have a plan for his team, but actually he would be only announcing a nonsensical summary of an aggregate of plans.

In order to press home this illustration, let us see wherein lies exactly the impossibility of conducting a hundred games of chess by central direction. Why would it be absurd to make one person responsible for the moves of all castles, another for all bishops, etc.? The answer is that the moving of any particular castle or bishop constitutes "a move in chess" only in the context of the moves (and possible moves) of the other pieces in the same game. It ceases to be "a move in chess" and is consequently meaningless in the context of the moves of all castles, or of all bishops, in a hundred different games. Such a context is a senseless collocation, falsely described as a purpose; whence the absurdity of entrusting a person with carrying out this fictitious purpose.

In effect, the absurdity of the statement: "The plan of this team is to move 45 pawns, 20 bishops, 15 castles, etc.," lies in three facts: (1) it regards several moves in each game of chess independently of their context and thus refers to entities which —in this context—are meaningless; (2) it collocates these meaningless entities to a (necessarily meaningless) aggregate and (3) it refers to this aggregate as to a purposeful action. More generally speaking, the manager's statement is absurd for it describes as a coherent action an irrelevant collocation of the meaningless fragments of several coherent actions.

All this can be said also of an overall economic plan, which announces as a national purpose an aggregate of various outputs. The figures listed in such a plan (such as tons of wheat to be harvested, barrels of oil to be refined, passengers to be transported) represent the sum of the outputs of several plants. When these outputs are thus added up, they are taken out of their economic context and regarded merely as processes of physical change. But the physical operation of a plant is in itself not a "process of production" at all, any more than the physical process of moving a chessman is in itself a "move in chess." (A plant, when working regardless of market conditions, would almost certainly be found—when brought into its proper economic context—to be operating destructively rather than productively.) The forming of aggregates of economically indeterminate operations is again meaningless—the sum of the output of two plants for example is no more a rational entity than the move of two castles in two games of chess.

Therefore (though with certain qualifications to be mentioned presently) for any national body to aim at a total of so many bushels of wheat harvested, or barrels of oil refined, or passenger miles travelled, or at any of the other items of production which fill the columns of an overall economic plan, is without any meaning. A particular sum of outputs could be rationally desired only in view of the reasons which make individual managers decide, after weighing up all alternative lines of production, on the sizes of the individual outputs constituting the sum. But the adding up of individual outputs to a production target eliminates all the proper reasons for which the individual plant managers might decide to produce such outputs as would add up to the totals set out in the plan, and there is then no reason left why these totals should be desired, nor any sense in planning them to be of any particular size.

If, nevertheless, production targets for wheat, oil, or transport of passengers, etc., do not sound as absurd as the proposed sum of pawns and castles to be moved by a team of chess-players, this is due to the presence in this case of a measure of rationality which, though quite insufficient to justify central economic planning, helps to cover up its fundamental absurdity.

167

First, while in general it is quite irrational to aim at any particular production target, there exist special conditions, for example in wartime, when almost every alternative to certain desired lines of production may be disregarded, and hence a production target may be rationally set out of so many tanks or aeroplanes. Actually even in wartime the method of thinking in aggregate targets, though indispensable, is fraught with the danger of irrational consequences. The rival pursuits of a number of targets will obstruct each other in a thousand unexpected ways and the allocation of resources to alternative targets will eventually have to take place in a scramble of competing departments, between whose rival claims no rational choice can be made and who are therefore reduced to snapping up and hoarding whatever resources they can lay hands on. However, there may be no better way of conducting large-scale production of extreme urgency in wartime, and the system of targets is therefore justified in these conditions.

Secondly, however irrational it may normally be to aim at production targets, the sums of goods produced are not in themselves meaningless. Given the functioning of an international self-adjusting order of distribution, which ascribes a world-price to each type of commodity—thus defining the rate at which each is voluntarily exchanged for any other type of commodity—we may regard the total price of the aggregate national product as a measure of national prosperity. It will reflect the standard of living of the people and also measure their military potential. And of course, there exist policies which may raise these national assets and it is rational to devise such policies and pursue them.

Governments committed to economic planning will embark to the full on every line of action that offers occasions —even though not entirely rational occasions—for some form of central intervention. In extreme cases, like that of the Soviets, the government may undertake to finance the whole of industry and keep check on its operations by a kind of ubiquitous Treasury Control. Extensive governmental investments and the responsibility for keeping plants in operation, will tend to produce inflation and necessitate widespread price controls, which will add to the economic responsibility of the State.[28]

The columns of figures set out in governmental economic plans express claims to economic powers that are only imaginary. But belief in such powers may be induced by carrying out with great emphasis some fairly extensive economic policies—which cause a certain amount of stress and strain—and pretending that you are thereby putting into effect your economic plan, with all its figures. This procedure follows the common practice of magic ritual. By draping yourself in black cloth, you attract dark clouds and by sprinkling water you make the rain come down. The absence of practical results does not disturb those who believe in magic, and the same is true for those who believe in economic planning. This is notoriously so for Russian planners and has been strikingly exposed also for their British counterparts by J. Jewkes in his *Ordeal by Planning*.

28. Comp. my *Full Employment and Free Trade* (1945), pp. 67–78.

9

Profits and Polycentricity[1]

Right through the course of history we can trace a wide-spread moral protest against the pursuit of commercial profits. To-day the abhorrence of the profit system among Socialists is perhaps the strongest political motive of our time. Yet somehow profit-seeking seems always to persist in spite of this. Even in Socialist Russia profits have turned up again, only slightly camouflaged by names like "planned surplus," "director's fund," etc.

I respect the moral resistance against profits as a great historical force, which has much humanized the system of money-making in the course of the past hundred years, and I think there is a great deal more to be done in that direction. But I consider the Socialist desire to eliminate commercial profits as the principal guide to economic activity to be profoundly mistaken. There exists no radical alternative to the capitalist system. "Planned production for commu-

1. *Humanitas,* 1946.

nity consumption" is a myth.[2] While the State must continue to canalize, correct and supplement the forces of the market, it cannot replace them to any considerable extent.

SUBSISTENCE FARMING. The most primitive manifestation of profit lies in the chance of a bumper harvest to the farmer subsisting directly on the fruits of his land. The lucky farmer gets something for nothing. But no one objects to such primitive profits. Their recipient may be envied, but hardly reproached.

Perhaps some may grumble at the farmer's investment policy; at the way he takes away part of the crop to increase stock piles, or to convert it into even more permanent forms by raising more livestock or by feeding with it his labourers employed on new constructions. However, within small groups of cultivators these troubles can be largely avoided by joint ownership and common management, as shown by the experience of communities of the kind of the Chaluzim in Palestine and of other Socialist settlers.

MONEY. Serious objections against profits arise only in more advanced societies, when the number of people who co-operate in producing goods for each other's use becomes very large. Profits, in these circumstances, are always in money and the fact which requires explanation before all is that money is being used for the exchange of goods.

---

2. The phrase is quoted from the Resolution adopted by the Labour Party Conference of 1942. Other characteristic statements in the Interim Report of the Executive to the Conference are: ". . . common ownership will alone secure the priority of national over private need which assures the community the power over its economic future"; ". . . an ugly scramble for profit in which there is no serious attempt to assess, in any coherent way, the priorities of national need." ". . . planned production in the service of the abundance that was open to us."

Why money? We must have an answer to this before we can discuss profits.

The reasons why money is used have often been given, but—it would seem to me—never with sufficient scope to account fully for the incidence and the important functions of profits. There are actually at least four distinct reasons for the use of money and only all four together can make profits properly intelligible.

CONSUMPTION. Reason A.1: When millions of people produce goods for each other's use, they must have some way of notifying each other of their desires. People's wants are very largely of a subjective nature. A man who wants his lunch looks exactly like a man who has had his, and it would take a very elaborate clinical examination to distinguish objectively between the two. Still less can you distinguish between the vegetarian and the non-vegetarian, or the man who prefers mashed potatoes from the other who likes them boiled. But it is easy to recognize the hungry man with all his personal preferences by the fact that he offers to buy a lunch and to pay for certain dishes.

Moreover, people's desires and preferences are fluctuating, complex and delicate. James Joyce could have filled a fat volume in describing the half-formed inclinations in the mind of a woman setting out on a shopping expedition. No words could completely define her potential desires. Consumers cannot therefore be expected to present shopkeepers with an adequate psychological analysis of their needs. Money comes to their rescue. Their offer to buy certain things at certain prices completely reveals what they have in mind.

Buying is, of course, often unwise. Moreover, for reasons to which I shall refer later, rationing becomes necessary in the case of sudden shortages, as for instance in war-time. These facts have served as arguments in favour of a maximum of rationing to ensure an enlightened and equitable distribution of goods. Against this there have been anxious and angry protests, exposing the clumsy and oppressive nature of a system of general rationing. While I fully agree with these protests, I shall not echo them here; firstly because I do not think that any government is likely to carry very far in practice the coercion of consumers by rationing, and secondly—what is more important—too much emphasis on this point would tend to overshadow the even weightier reasons for which money is needed to run a modern economy.

Reason A.2: Even if there were no difficulty whatever in establishing the inclinations of people to satisfy their wants, there would still remain a big problem to be solved for a rational distribution of goods. Perhaps we can make this clear by imagining for a moment that men were robots, i.e. machines functioning exactly like men. They would require to be fed by a multitude of varied goods and sustained by a great many different services, exactly like ordinary human beings; but they should show an improvement on human beings by carrying a gauge which records at every moment the precise degree to which their needs are satisfied. This would entirely eliminate the function of money as a medium of expression for subjective, delicate and complex desires, so that the task of distributing provisions to the population would become purely a matter of engineering. And yet—I maintain—there would still be no way of carrying out this task rationally without the use of money.

A rigorous proof of this assertion cannot be attempted here for it would take us too far into mathematics; but I shall at least try to outline the argument.[3]

The following preliminary considerations may be useful. A robot being similar to a human being, it can be equally sat-

3. The impossibility of solving rigorously a "polycentric" problem, i.e. involving the mutual adjustment of a large number of centres, is referred to in some mathematical detail on pp. 211 and 224–25.

isfied (to the same mark on his gauge) by an infinite variety of articles offered to him. Therefore any particular distribution of a definite batch of goods between two robots—say robots Number One and Two—will in general be capable of improvement. It will be possible to readjust it so as to produce greater satisfaction both for One and Two (or at least one of them, while leaving that of the other unchanged). This teaches us how to define a rational distribution of goods. We may say that when the distribution of the available goods between all robots is such that it is not possible to increase the gauge reading of any without depressing that of another, then that distribution is *rational.*

By analysing the possibility of exchanges between robots in such a rational or "balanced" state of affairs, it can be shown that a definite exchange ratio prevails in it for every kind of goods. Hence, in a "balanced" state the value of commodities can be fixed in terms of money. We have only to fix arbitrarily the value of one single piece of goods—say a certain pot of jam—to be equal to 1s. But the problem of rational distribution has yet to be defined more closely. Some assumption must be made about the "income distribution" between robots. This point can be readily disposed of by deciding, for example, on a system of complete equality which allocates shares of identical value to each robot.

We have now defined our problem. Next we shall outline the method of *successive approximation* by which such problems can be solved.[4]

We want to find the distribution of available resources which will maximize the sum total of gauge readings for all robots (their respective shares being of equal value). A procedure of successive approximations will divide such a problem into an indefinitely extended series of successive stages.

4. This method is discussed further on pp. 212–13.

Only one centre will be considered at a time and adjusted in relation to all the others, while the mutual interrelations of these is taken as fixed for the moment. One centre after another will be singled out and the solution thus further re-adjusted at each step. When a complete set of such adjustments covering all centres will have been carried out, each centre may be once more re-adjusted, taking into account the adjustments made meanwhile at other centres. Whole sets of successive approximations may thus repeatedly be carried out and the total solution rendered more and more accurate. Such is the general method of approximation by which a "polycentric" problem of the kind under consideration can be solved, if it can be solved at all.

A particular form of this general method is found to apply to our problem. It proceeds as follows. We start by ascribing a price to each item of the available supplies—trying to guess as closely as possible at the value which it will have in a "balanced" state of distribution. The total of prices divided by the number of robots is then regarded as the "claim" of each robot. This claim represents in effect a sum of money in respect to which the robot's share of goods will be allocated to it. Turning now to Robot Number One we start off on the process of distribution by doing on its behalf what an individual shopper would do. We assign to the robot a pile of provisions which gives it the greatest satisfaction (as measured on its gauge) within the scope of its quota of purchasing power. Next we proceed to spend step by step each robot's money to the best of its advantage. But as we go on, we have to modify the "prices" so as to make certain that eventually supply meets demand, which necessarily leads to a revaluation of the piles previously allocated. So we have to go back again to each past allocation and somewhat re-adjust it. In effect—to cut a long story short—the procedure will be equivalent to giving each robot an equal sum of money and making it buy its provisions to the best of its satisfaction at the public stores; the prices of commodities being adjusted at the level which equates current supply with current demand.

Such is Reason A.2, for the use of money: money is indispensable as a medium for adjusting a multitude of claims to a maximum of total satisfaction.

I shall now pass on to the sphere of production, where we shall meet very similar situations requiring the use of money. Their discussion will throw further light, by analogy, on what has just been said.

PRODUCTION. Consider thousands of factories in which millions of people are at work. Each factory selects from an immensely varied reservoir of resources a particular assortment of materials and grades of labour. It applies certain technical processes suitable to its particular circumstances. It keeps readjusting its requirements of resources and its methods of production, to adapt itself to changes in the nature of supplies and in the demands of consumers.

Each factory is entrusted to a manager who is responsible for its operations. The success of the economic system depends on the managers doing their task well. But nobody can do a task well unless he knows what it consists in. And, if it involves using up labour and other scarce resources and producing at the expense of these resources goods for other people, it is desirable that there should be some check kept on the way the task is carried out. This should preferably be exercised by the prospective users of the resultant products, who should be empowered to make sure that the maximum possible advantage has been extracted from the total of utilized resources.

Hence Reason B.1 for the use of money. Business accounts cast up in money are a scoring-board to which managers can look for guidance in directing their efforts and which will also afford the basis for outside control over their activities. The score consists in the amount of money received for sales, less the amount spent on buying resources. The first sum is the measure, and—as we have seen in the previous section—the only practicable measure, of the satisfaction given to consumers, and hence it is reasonable that it should be made a maximum. The second sum is, as we shall presently show, the only practicable measure for the cost of production, which obviously should be reduced to a minimum.

When people write poetry, or teach a child to read and write, or restore a patient's eyesight by removing a cataract, their actions will carry much of their own reward in them. Those who feel they have done well in such matters can dispense with outside recognition or else demand it as of right. But this is not so for the production of shoe-laces, tooth brushes, razors, etc., which is a satisfying occupation too, but not in itself. It satisfies you only if you are sure that you produce what is wanted: what is giving satisfaction to others. Therefore you must measure your satisfaction in terms of theirs. And insofar as their satisfaction is measurable by their willingness to pay for your produce, you must aim at making as much money as possible on your sales. This will represent the proper way of assessing managerial achievements and will also offer the proper control over the manager by those whom he serves. This kind of control can easily be equipped with effective sanctions. The rewards of the manager can be readily made dependent on his takings from sales, be it in form of a premium or of promotion, etc. No system of managerial rewards will be rational if it does not take for its guide the manager's capacity of making money.

I have purposely omitted in this paper any discussion of economic justice. In the great civilizations of the past, incomes were grossly unequal; much more so, it would seem, than under capitalism. The trend towards greater equality has been maintained throughout the last hundred years—and particularly accentuated in this country since 1939. I am convinced (and have elaborated this in my book *Full Employment and Free Trade*) that a system of capitalistic enterprise can be made to conform in this respect to any standard of social justice on which society is sufficiently agreed. There is no necessary reason why profits should lead to economic injustice.

It is obviously reasonable that production should be conducted at a minimum cost in terms of utilized resources. And this is not, in general, simply a question of using less of everything. More often it presents itself in form of a choice, whether to use, say, less coal and less oil and use instead more labour and capital, plus perhaps a different quality of coal. Balances of a similar kind have often to be struck in other fields than industrial production, for example by artists or athletes. Or again by doctors prescribing a cure, or by designers of machinery; or—approaching closely the case of industrial production—by farmers subsisting on their own land. In all these cases the persons practising economy can strike a balance between sacrifices and achievements, which they can directly sense and weigh. But the factory manager who gets his resources supplied from outside, cannot feel directly how precious each parcel of it is from the point of view of society as a whole. He must have some external objective criterion in terms of which he can balance their alternative utilization; in other words, if he is to use his resources rationally, he must be supplied with a numerical valuation for each available particle of resources. These numerical values must be expressed in money. In order to prove this, I have to pass on to Reason B.2 for the use of money.

Reason B.2 will be seen to be closely analogous to Reason A.2. It arises from the circumstance that thousands of factory managers are offered millions of parcels of resources (particularly labour and natural resources) and have to find the best way of utilizing the lot.

Let us assume (to simplify our task) that we have no serious difficulty in calculating in advance the amount of satisfaction—in terms of total sales at given prices—which will result from any particular distribution of resources among the existing factories. The problem of maximizing this total is then almost the same as that of maximizing the total satisfaction of robots by an appropriate distribution of provisions among them. And again, the problem is, in general, quite insoluble except by some method of successive approximation which considers one centre (i.e. one factory) at a time and disregards meanwhile the interrelations between all the others.

Fortunately, in this case the "satisfaction" produced at the several centres is expressed from the start in the same units—namely money. That greatly simplifies matters and makes possible a solution on the following lines. Each factory to be supplied with as much money as it requires, provided that it repays it at the end of a cycle of production and sale. Factories to be enjoined to purchase at the public stores such resources, the utilization of which will lead to most profitable sales. Each parcel of resources to go by auction to the factory which can make best use of it. It is implied here that the resources are at the disposal of some persons—called here "Producers"—who will sell them to the highest bidder.[5] That, in particular, labour will seek the highest wage and that land and other natural resources will similarly be brought to market as profitably as possible by their owners. That is an integral part of the method.

No other method than this—or some close variant of it—can be used which would be even approximately as rational in allocating resources to a large number of produc-

5. In the outline on p. 198 below, these persons are called W = workers; L = landowners; I = investors.

tive centres. Therefore "money-making" by "Producers," who will sell resources to Managers and by Managers who will utilize them and sell the produce to the Consumers, is indispensable to the achievement of such an allocation.

This is Reason B.2 for the use of money. It clearly brings us quite close to the discussion of profits; but we are not yet quite ready for this.

THE CIRCULATION OF MONEY.   The money which factory managers receive on loan for the purchase of resources, is paid out by them to the Producers and received back by them from the Consumers. This forms the circulation of money. The managers are its heart: they squirt the money into every particle of the social body in payment of its contribution to production—and they receive it back again from all these quarters in return for the sale of finished products. The outgoing streams serve to allocate resources to factories, etc.; the incoming streams guide the produce to the users. By avoiding losses, the managers keep the whole process under control. The money which they receive for their own services and spend again as consumers, forms a little separate circulation like that of the coronary system of the heart. By this extension of our scheme, managers are included among "Producers."

Producers and Consumers are of course the same people, and form in effect the whole population. The devices of monetary circulation and money-making offer to the population the only possible way of rationally co-operating in the common exploitation of a pool of varied resources, for the production of a large variety of goods destined for distribution among themselves.

STATIC CONDITIONS.   Yet if only production and distribution went on unchanged day after day, there would be no need to keep up the circulation of money. Circulation could then be used to start the system off in the right way, and be abandoned thereafter. Something of the kind happens whenever monetary methods are abandoned for some reason, in some part of the economic process. The schedules of production and distribution prevailing up to that time are usually adopted as standards for further operations. The "basic" rations of paper, for example, are still related in Britain to-day to the amount which publishers happened to use in 1939, when the commercial guides of production were first superseded by war-time controls. While completely static conditions of production would make the use of money unnecessary, the opposite extreme of large sudden changes may cause a temporary breakdown of the monetary mechanism. For example, when in the last war most of the natural rubber production of the world fell into Japanese hands, the Allied Governments were forced to confiscate all available rubber supplies. The alternative course of paying sufficiently high prices to induce holders of rubber stocks to sell these to munition factories rather than to private persons (for tyres, office floors, etc.), would have created enormous unearned incomes to the stock holders, which the public was not prepared to tolerate.

The fact that it is useful to ration certain commodities in exceptional circumstances does not affect our argument, which denies the possibility of a central allocation of resources to factories and of products to consumers. For apart from a few cases, like the distribution of milk to schoolchildren and cod-liver oil to expectant mothers, rationing is purely a clumsy imitation of distributive schedules established previously by commerce. Its clumsiness is due to the fact that such a schedule cannot be reasonably continued in operation for any length of time. This applies with particular force to a schedule of productive resources. Any attempt to enforce a rigid central allocation of all resources of production (labour, raw materials, machinery, land) to factories, would lead therefore to an almost immediate standstill of the whole system of production.

WHY PROFITS?   This brings us to the heart of our question. I have described an economic system based on money-making. In such a system people are often making gains which they have done little or nothing to earn. Whenever anything that I possess becomes scarce, whether through increased demand or otherwise—be it my special type of skill or a commodity which I have in stock or which I can readily produce on my land or in my factory—I inevitably make a profit on it. Similarly, as a consumer, I make unearned money if the price of the loaf or of electric light goes down. The economic system is constantly readjusted by the incidence of such profits—and by the losses which occur with about equal frequency at other points.

I have already said that in extreme instances, particularly in times of great national emergency, measures are taken to eliminate the occasion for earning large profits from sudden scarcities. I can well imagine that public conscience may in future become increasingly watchful in such matters and I think there is still much scope for it. Besides, my outline of a money-making society is not yet complete, and I shall have a number of qualifications to introduce and supplementary points to add.

I have insisted that modern production and distribution can be organized only on commercial lines, but I have said nothing to suggest that such a solution is perfect. If somebody insists that you need an engine to pull a train (as against people who would press for running trains by the method of scenic railways), he must not be taken to deny that the efficiency of engines is very limited; that they make a noise and sometimes run over people—such points being quite irrelevant to the proposition that you need an engine to pull a train. And I would add, that it is impossible to deal rationally with any of the troubles caused by engines, until you cease hankering after trains without them.

SOCIAL REPERCUSSIONS.   There are millions of things which people buy, use up, and that is the end of it. But this is not always so. Not for example when they buy education or shrubs for their front gardens. People who acquire knowledge or lay out attractive gardens do not reduce to the same extent other people's share of such things, for the benefits they acquire are transmitted to a certain degree to others around them. Similar "diffuse" effects of individual economic acts—most of them undesirable—are very common in the sphere of production. Smoke, noise, river pollution, soil erosion, depletion of fish and game, industrial ill-health, moral frustration of the industrial worker and many other instances come to the mind. The money-making system of economy is based on the assumption that such diffuse effects are negligible; that each individual step makes a circumscribed and visible contribution (positive or negative) to the common welfare and that the score of total welfare is arrived at by adding up the scores for each step. In other words, money-making organizes those aspects of economic life which are atomistic, localizable and additive, and leaves uncontrolled its "diffuse" or "social" aspects.

Wherever these repercussions become prominent, there is a case for action by the public authorities, who are ultimately responsible for social welfare. The question is: what can they do? In the light of our argument which denies the possibility of any central direction of economic life, public interventions will have to be negative rather than prescriptive. They will largely consist in restricting the range of commercial activities by outlawing unsocial transactions. Here lies the great field of social reform in which the last hundred years have made such decisive contributions to civilization. In addition to this, in a number of distinctive cases the State will undertake important positive actions, making provisions for education, health and social amenities, which are insufficiently or unsatisfactorily supplied by commercial sources. Yet for all this, the major part of production and consumption will remain—and must remain—directed in its particulars by a money-making system, which ignores the "diffuse" effects of its own activities. The government can restrain such a system and correct it here and there by special taxes and subsidies, and it will supplement it by public services; but there exists no organizing principle which will maximize the "diffuse" advantages at which such measures are aiming, with anything remotely approaching the effectiveness with which money-making maximizes the total of "localizable" advantages and minimizes "localizable" costs. A modern industrial system can therefore be rationally conducted only as long as the majority of costs are circumscribed, its products suitable for distribution to individual consumers and are fully used up by those who acquire them.[6]

I shall return to this point once more when referring to Nationalization.

PREVENTION OF UNEMPLOYMENT. I have described the circulation of money. How the managers pay out money to "Producers" in exchange for labour and other resources, and how the money then comes back to them from the same people, spending it as Consumers in exchange for finished goods. (A small branch of the circulation being passed through the managers' pockets to pay for their services.) I have said that the managers must recover the whole of the money which they put into circulation, for the money is supposed to be only on loan with them. I may mention also that if they fail in this matter, they are compelled to close down and sell out.

Actually, Consumers do not usually spend their whole income, but prefer to set aside some of it to increase their fund

6. See p. 235 below.

of security. Thus managers may fall short of recovering all the money they have put into circulation and according to the rules of commercial management, this may force a number of them out of business. Trade would become depressed and there would be unemployment. It is true that the effects of private saving may be offset to a greater or lesser extent by money laid out by managers (from loans) for the construction of new factories. But in prosperous communities at an advanced state of industrialization, this will usually not be sufficient fully to offset savings and a state of chronic depression will tend to prevail. Fortunately these troubles can be remedied by governmental deficit spending. Far from representing an "incurable internal contradiction of Capitalism" (as Socialist literature still maintains), chronic unemployment is due to an incidental defect of the capitalist system, which could be eliminated merely by setting aside certain long exploded prejudices concerning the conduct of public finance.

NATIONALIZATION. So far I have said almost nothing about ownership. I have mentioned that some of the "Producers" are owners of land and other natural resources, and have hinted at some source whence managers receive their business capital on loan. Since the construction of new factories would be paid for from such loans, the ownership of factories may be presumed to be held by the lenders, who would be investing their money in return for a share in profits. But this still leaves it open whether ownership in any of the cases mentioned is private or public; which seems to indicate that it makes—or should make—little difference which it is.

The essential difference between private enterprise and public ownership of industry lies in the way risks are borne in the two cases. In the first case, it is left to private individuals to subscribe business capital or give loans to managers. They keep watch on the investment market and try to shift their capital always into the most promising fields. Thus they tend to achieve its best utilization. As a reward they earn a share in profits, minus, of course, the burden of occasional losses. Moreover, they are entitled to interest on loans and to repayment of capital; to assure this, they are given the right to foreclose on a defaulting debtor. When the State becomes the sole investor it could behave in a way which would result in very nearly the same state of affairs. Sums available for investment could be handed out to a number of individual agents, who could be remunerated from the profits and interests earned by them. They would differ from private capitalists only in being prevented from eating into their capital and not being allowed to transmit it to their heirs. But neither of these features would noticeably affect the mechanism of the economic system. State ownership will, of course, weigh more heavily if the State decides—as in Soviet Russia —to act as a holding company for all industrial enterprises, providing them centrally with capital both on long and short terms, and participating in their profits as well as bearing their losses. This eliminates the capital market as a means of re-distributing investments and replaces its method of "successive approximation" by the cruder central decision of a government department. At the same time the watch kept on the solvency of enterprise is relaxed, as vigilance ceases to be backed by any effective threat of foreclosure.

These economic consequences of state-ownership are not unimportant and the pooling of all savings in the hands of the State may have also far-reaching political consequences. Yet the striking fact to notice is, in view of Socialist expectations of "planned production for community consumption," that State-ownership makes in reality so little difference. I expressed this a few pages back in rather abstract terms, which will be further expanded in the subsequent essay. At this point I only want to indicate my final conclusions, without claiming to have strictly proven them.

PROFITS AND POLYCENTRICITY

Let the industrial system of a nation be composed of one hundred thousand productive centres, each drawing on the same market of industrial resources and supplying with its produce the same market of finished (or semi-finished) goods; each centre to be directed by a manager, who under private capitalism is nominated by the shareholders and under public ownership is appointed by the government. Under capitalism the manager is responsible to the shareholders for making profit, while the government controls the conditions under which profits are made. I suggest that under State-ownership the situation is not materially different. The government (like the shareholders) must find some administrative means of controlling the managers whom it has appointed. Only by applying some general rules, can a government exercise control over a large number of persons whose task is determined by relations directly established between them. It must lay down definite criteria of efficiency, which must be binding on itself in the sense that any manager who fulfils them could claim to have done his duty and to receive recognition for this. The criteria must be precise and easily recognizable, for otherwise they would place a premium on wangling and tend to penalize the honest scorer. The only precise and rational criterion of managerial success that can be found is the test of business profits. And once a summary test of this kind is imposed and accepted as a measure of his efficiency, the manager must be given full discretion as to the means of achieving it, within the general rules laid down for his operations. The position then coincides with that under private capitalism.

It is a mistake which lingers persistently even when this situation is accepted, to assume that the government controlling the managers appointed by itself, can fashion more detailed rules for their control than when dealing with private managers. The administrative limitations are the same in both cases. In both cases the government can make its preferences felt and can modify the profit criterion in their sense. It can grant premiums and impose fines or special taxes, but in either case these measures must be based on the same kind of data: of a kind that is swiftly and reliably endorsable by an accountant's certificate. State-ownership of industry can make but little difference to the operations of the economic machinery. In its legitimate efforts to assure those interests of society which the money-making machinery leaves out of account (as well as in trying to eliminate monopolistic exploitation, etc.), a socialist government will be limited to the use of the same, or very similar, instruments of administration by which any government today can control private industry.

Much of the confusion and internal tension of Soviet Russia is due to the desperate reluctance to admit this. It results in ever-renewed and often violent attempts to exercise more specific control over the machinery of economic life than is compatible with the rules of an effectively functioning system of production.

To sum up, there exists no fundamental alternative to the system of money-making and profit-seeking. Our modern high-standard economy was built up on this system and its elimination would reduce our economy to the level of subsistence farming. In practice, this would mean the extinction of all the highly industrialized nations of the West. Instead of hankering after the myth of "planned production for community consumption," we must proceed further with the reform of our commercial system. The last century of reform has already humanized capitalist society far beyond earlier hopes. We shall advance even more rapidly and smoothly in future, if we fully recognize at last that we must take our stand on this system and improve and develop its possibilities.

10

Manageability of Social Tasks

Part I

Mainly Descriptive

My argument for freedom in science bears a close resemblance to the classical doctrine of economic individualism. The scientists of the world are viewed as a team setting out to explore the existing openings for discovery and it is claimed that their efforts will be efficiently co-ordinated if—and only if—each is left to follow his own inclinations.[1] This statement is very similar to Adam Smith's claim with regard to a team of business men, drawing on the same market of productive resources for the purpose of satisfying different parts of the same system of demand. Their efforts—he said—would be co-ordinated, as by an invisible hand, to the most economical utilization of the available resources.

These two systems of maximized utility are indeed based on similar principles; and more than that: they are only two examples of a whole set of parallel cases. There is a wide range of such systems in nature exhibiting similar types of order. They have been called systems of "dynamic order" by

1. See above p. 41 and further throughout Part 1.

Köhler, whose designation I followed in an earlier writing;[2] but I think it will be simpler to refer to them as systems of *spontaneous order.*

TWO KINDS OF ORDER[3]

Wherever we see a well-ordered arrangement of things or men, we instinctively assume that someone has intentionally placed them in that way. A well-kept garden must have been laid out; a machine working properly must have been constructed and a company on parade must have been drilled and placed under command: that is the obvious way for order to emerge. Such a method of establishing order consists in limiting the freedom of things and men to stay or move about at their pleasure, by assigning to each a specific position in a prearranged plan.

But there exists another, less obviously determined type of order which is based on the opposite principle. The water in a jug settles down, filling the hollow of the vessel perfectly and in even density, up to the level of a horizontal plane which forms its free surface: a perfect arrangement such as no human artifice could reproduce, should the process of gravitation and cohesion, to which it is due, refuse to function for a moment. Yet any number of such containers of varied and complex shapes, joined to a system of communicating vessels, could be filled in the same perfect and uniform way up to a common horizontal plane—merely by letting a liquid come to rest in them.

In this second type of order no constraint is applied specifically to the individual particles; the forces from outside, like the resistance of the vessels and the forces of gravitation, take effect in an entirely indiscriminate fashion. The

2. "The Growth of Thought in Society" (*Economica*, 1941, p. 428).

3. The contents of this section are taken from my article in *Economica* loc. cit.

particles are thus free to obey the internal forces acting between them, and the resultant order represents the equilibrium between all the internal and external forces.

If outside forces are absent or negligible and the internal forces operate alone, the resulting equilibria present even more striking regularities. Fluids, gases and liquids take on spherical shapes and at lower temperatures substances solidify into crystals, in which the atoms are arrayed at faultlessly even intervals in the three dimensions of space.

The molecules of half a dozen different substances, dissolved together in a glass of hot water, will deposit on cooling within a few minutes, each substance building up separate crystals of its own. Many millions of molecules of each will be sorted out from the others and neatly stacked up in their separate, regularly spaced piles. The achievement may be assessed in its magnitude by imagining the sorting out, and careful arrangement into separate regular stacks of the differently coloured marbles of a layer covering the whole planet. Such a task would keep the whole of humanity busy for years; yet a similar result is accomplished spontaneously in a few seconds, by the internal forces acting between the molecules.

It is clear that the intervention of any human agency which attempted to take over the task of such internal forces would be entirely inadequate. If the particles had to wait to be picked out and placed into position individually, the authorities assuming responsibility for ordering them would, in fact, merely compel them to remain in disorder indefinitely. This seems to suggest that when very large numbers are to be arranged carefully, it can be achieved only by the spontaneous mutual adjustment of the units, not by assignment of the several units to specifically prescribed positions.

A spontaneously attained order can be most delicate and complex. The growth and form of plants and animals are instances of such order. The evolution of a polycellular organism from the fertilized cell may be regarded as arising from the continuous tendency of its particles, interacting with the nutrient medium, to come to an internal equilibrium. The cells within the field of one embryonic "organizer" have in fact the capacity—proved by mutilating or transplanting experiments—to play any part that may fall to them through the interplay of the internal forces within the area. The entire evolution of species is commonly thought to have resulted from a continued process of internal equilibration in living matter, under varying outside circumstances.

But this should not prejudice us in favour of order by mutual adjustment, and against specifically planned order. Where smaller numbers are concerned, the latter is likely to show a greatly superior performance: all machinery and mechanical technique of man demonstrates this superiority when the numbers are small enough. The two alternative and opposite methods of achieving order—by limiting the freedom of the particles, or by giving full scope to their interactions—have their respective proper occasions. Unless one of these methods is preferred for its own sake (for instance "planners" insisting on deliberate direction, or adherents of *laissez-faire* on the use of automatism) it should in general be easy to decide which task can be accomplished by one and which by the other. They will combine in the way mutually exclusive functions combine, namely each fitting into a gap left open by the other.

We must keep in mind also that, as a rule, there will be no such mutual interaction between units of an aggregate which would arrange them in a desired orderly fashion. Mutual forces, like those operating between molecules or the cells of an organism, might be absent altogether, as in the case of the differently coloured marbles which have no tendency to segregate spontaneously. Or again, the spontaneously established order may be undesirable, for example when a chemical reaction, performed in an unfavourable medium, yields unwanted products; or when a morbid growth kills an organism.

This suggests that, while it may be possible to achieve certain socially desirable forms of co-ordination in society by allowing each individual to adjust his action to that of all the others (or to some state of affairs resulting from the action of all the others) there is no warrant to assume either (1) that any particular conceivable task of co-ordination can be attained by such a technique or (2) that any particular instance of free mutual adjustment between individuals will produce a desirable result. It warns us that even the most wonderful successes achieved by such adjustment will not be free of manifest shortcomings nor represent more than a relative optimum. But it suggests, nevertheless, that such tasks as a system of free adjustment may achieve, cannot be effectively performed by any other technique of co-ordination.

PRIVATE FREEDOM

An earlier essay in this series, *The Span of Central Direction,* dealt in some detail with the methods of establishing deliberate order in society and attempted to prove their complete inadequacy in coping with tasks achieved by spontaneous order. My main subject here is to survey and roughly to analyse the principal systems of spontaneous order in society. But before turning to this, I must mention a class of individualistic manifestations which do not contribute to any system of spontaneous order in society. There are many things an individual can do which have negligible social effects; or—to be precise—the social effects of which are considered negligible by the authorities as well as by the consensus of opinion throughout society. The range of the things he can thus do of his own free will and without danger of incurring punishment or censure is important and it is also true that the range of such private individualism is not unrelated to the scope of public liberties. In a condition of serfdom or villeinage, private freedom and public liberty are jointly reduced to zero. And liberation from such unfreedom is gained by the establishment of public liberties, both legal and commercial. To quote Bracton: "For that is an absolute villeinage from which an uncertain and indeterminate service is rendered, where it cannot be known in the evening what service is to be rendered in the morning, that is where a person is bound to whatever is enjoined to him." The first step towards liberation is the fixing of feudal dues by custom, law or written copy. And finally, by commutation of these dues in terms of money, the copyholder becomes a tenant, entitled to dispose freely of his own time and person, and to select according to his own judgment what is most congenial and profitable for him to do.

But the scope of public liberties is not generally proportional to that of private freedom. The two may even be inversely related. Private nihilism prepares the mind for submission to public despotism; and a despotic regime may continue to tolerate unrestrained forms of private life, which another society living under public freedom would have stamped out by social ostracism. Under Stalin the scope of private freedom remains much wider than it was in Victorian Britain, while that of public liberties is incomparably less.

A free society is characterized by the range of public liberties through which individualism performs a social function, and not by the scope of socially ineffective personal liberties. Conversely, totalitarianism is not intent on destroying private freedom, but denies all justification to public liberties. In the totalitarian conception, independent personal actions can never perform a social function, but can only satisfy a private desire; while all public responsibility falls to the state. The liberal conception of society which attributes a decisive part to the operation of individual freedom in the public life of nations, must recognize that this entails a distinction between two aspects of freedom: public and private. Both deserve protection; but it is damaging to the first that it should be demanded and its justification sought—as often happens—on the grounds of the second.

When order is achieved among human beings by allowing them to interact with each other on their own initiative—subject only to laws which uniformly apply to all of them—we have a system of spontaneous order in society. We may then say that the efforts of these individuals are co-ordinated by exercising their individual initiative and that this self-co-ordination justifies their liberty on public grounds.

The actions of such individuals are said to be free, for they are not determined by any *specific* command, whether of a superior or of a public authority; the compulsion to which they are subject is impersonal and general. There are dozens of aspects in which these individuals are not free. They are under compulsion to earn their living, they may be exploited by their employers, bullied by their families, deluded by their own vanity, and must all die; it is not claimed that they are free in any other sense than such as is expressly stated. How far such liberty is of intrinsic value and deserves protection, even apart from its social usefulness, is a question which I leave open at this stage and shall try to clarify later.

An aggregate of individual initiatives can lead to the establishment of spontaneous order only if each takes into account in its action what the others have done in the same context before. Where large numbers are involved, such mutual adjustment must be indirect; each individual adjusts himself to a state of affairs resulting from the foregoing actions of the rest. This requires that information about the state of affairs in question should be available to each member of the aggregate; as in the case of such communal states of affairs as the condition of various markets, the current achievements of scientific progress, or the position of the law up to date. We may add that for "individuals" we may read "corporations acting as individuals."

MARKETING SYSTEMS

The most massive example of spontaneous order in society —the prototype of order established by an "invisible hand" —is that of economic life based on an aggregate of competing individuals. I want to sketch out here its main features only so far as this is required for comparing this particular spontaneous system with others of a different character.

We shall take separately the system of producers and the system of consumers. To simplify matters we shall regard for the start all "producers" as plant managers, hiring or buying resources for the production of goods and services for sale to consumers. The persons from whom they hire or buy these resources (labour, land, capital) will be brought in later.

Producers are constantly on the look-out for an opening to utilize at a greater profit the resources which they control and to gain control over more resources, hitherto managed by other producers, by finding more profitable applications for them. Accordingly, each new decision of a producer will involve changes of his demands on the market of resources. Such demands are made publicly in terms of money which is used in common by everybody. Each new decision of a producer modifies therefore the prices on which the further decisions of all other producers will depend. Such are the mutual adjustments between the decisions of individual producers.

Each adjustment will tend to lessen the amount of resources required for producing a given satisfaction offered to consumers. Jointly they will tend to reduce total production costs to a minimum. The result is a state of order, for it forms an aggregate possessing an advantage by virtue of a particular collocation of varied and numerous elements. It is a spontaneously established order, for it originates in the independent actions of individuals, guided by a common situation previously created by the similarly guided independent actions of other individuals of the same group. It is a case of spontaneous order in society.

Before passing on to the consumers, let me make good some serious over-simplifications of this sketch. The managers (M) are of course bargaining for the resources of production with those who can dispose of them. We may take it that (in the absence of slavery) each worker (W) is entitled to dispose of his own labour. There will, moreover, be some persons whom we will call "landowners" (L) entitled to dispose commercially of land for use as factory sites, agriculture and other productive purposes and finally some investors (I) who will dispose of capital. The managers' dealings with the persons called W, L and I, will be carried out in separate markets, each of which is a system of spontaneous order, spontaneously adjusted to the other two.

Finally, on the other side (as it were) of the managers there are the consumers (C) so that the total picture in its simplest form is as follows—with double-arrows indicating market relations.

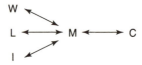

We now direct our attention to the system of adjustments prevailing between the managers (M) and the consumers (C). Consumers also set up a system of spontaneous order. The consecutive purchases of buyers, each of which is adjusted to the market conditions created by previous purchases, tends to produce a condition in which consumers are receiving—subject to the prevailing distribution of income—the maximum satisfaction of their preferences from the available goods and services. This system is supplemented by another system operating between the managers who compete for the demand of consumers.

The systems of spontaneous order (to the left of M) assuring production at a minimum cost, are linked to the systems of spontaneous order (to the right of M), assuring maximum satisfaction, by the fact that the consumers are the same people as the W, L, I and M. C represents the population as consumers, W, L, I and M the same population as producers. This situation has been referred to before (p. 180).

SYSTEMS OF INTELLECTUAL ORDER

Of the systems of spontaneous order which form part of the intellectual life of society I shall take first the example of Law, and in particular Common Law.

Consider a judge sitting in court and deciding a difficult case. While pondering his decision, he refers consciously to dozens of precedents and unconsciously to many more. Before him numberless other judges have sat and decided according to statute, precedent, equity and convenience, as he himself will have to decide now; his mind, while he analyses the various aspects of the case, is in constant contact with theirs. And beyond the purely legal references, he senses the entire contemporary trend of opinions, the social medium as a whole. Not until he has established all these bearings of his case and responded to them in the light of his own professional conscience, will his decision acquire force of conviction and will he be ready to declare it.

The moment this point is reached and the judgment announced, the tide starts running backwards. The addition made to the Law by the decision just taken may be massive or slight; in either case it represents an interpretation of the hitherto existing Law, reinforcing or modifying its system in some respect. It makes it appear henceforth in a somewhat new light. Public opinion too has received a new response and a new stimulus. Every new decision in court gives guidance to all future judges for their decisions of cases yet unthought of.

The operation of Common Law thus constitutes a sequence of adjustments between succeeding judges, guided by a parallel interaction between the judges and the general public. The result is the ordered growth of the Common Law, steadily re-applying and re-interpreting the same fundamental rules and expanding them thus to a system of increasing scope and consistency. Such coherence and fitness as this system possesses at any time is the direct embodiment of the wisdom with which each consecutive judicial decision is adjusted to all those made before and to any justified changes in public opinion.

Accordingly, the operations of a judicial system of case law is an instance of spontaneous order in society. But we see that it differs profoundly from the systems of production or consumption by the fact that it achieves more than temporal advantages. While an economic system of spontaneous order co-ordinates individual actions merely to serve the momentary material interest of its participants, an orderly process of judicature deposits a valid and lasting system of legal thought.

The next example of spontaneous order brings us back to the opening theme of this book, which is Science. Every scientist in search of discovery is faced with the scientific results and opinions of all other scientists up to that time, which are summed up in textbooks or—for more recent works—in current publications and public discussions. In the setting of his problem, in the way in which he pursues it and reaches his conclusions, he follows the recognized methods of science with such personal variations as he thinks fit to apply.

The scientist differs from the judge in that he is not given a case to decide, but has to select his own problem for investigation. Early in life he specializes on certain branches of science which seem to fit his inclinations, and then through the years of his apprenticeship in research he keeps looking out for some problem specially suited to his gifts, by the pursuit of which he may hope to achieve important results. Since the credit for a new discovery goes to the scientist who first publishes it, each will be eager to publish his results as soon as he feels sure of them. This induces scientists to inform their colleagues without delay of their current progress. On the other hand, sharp sanctions are in operation against premature publication, and scientists whose conclusions have proved hasty suffer a serious loss in reputation; this guards scientific opinion from being confused by a flood of erroneous claims put in circulation by too ambitious investigators. Every new claim put forward by a scientist is received with a measure of scepticism by the scientific public, and the author may find it necessary to defend his claim against possible objections. Thus every proposed addition to the body of science is subjected to a regular process of scrutiny, the arguments on both sides being given public hearing before scientific opinion decides to accept or reject the new ideas in question.

In the way a scientist, wrestling with a problem, accepts as his premise a great mass of previously established knowledge and submits to the guidance of scientific standards, while taking also into account the whole trend of current scientific opinion, he resembles a judge referring to precedent and statute and interpreting them in the light of contemporary thought. But in the way the scientist selects a new problem to which he might apply his gifts to the best advantage, and, when discovery is achieved, puts forward his claims as soon as he is certain of their validity, pressing for their acceptance by the scientific public—the scientist acts more like a business man, who first searches for a new profitable application of the resources at his disposal and then hastens to advertise and commend his products to the consumers before anyone can forestall him.

The first method of adjustment is common to judges and scientists and is a process of *consultation*. The consistent growth of law and science derives from the consultative acts by which the dynamic systems of law and science are maintained. Turning on the other hand to business men, we find few consultative contacts between them. Though commercial ideas also keep growing continuously, their cultivation is not the main function of a commercial system. Mutual adjustment between business men is primarily guided by a striving for individual advantage, and we have seen that the same applies in a modified form to some important aspects of scientific work. In both these cases we have a *competitive* adjustment which, wherever it operates, tends to maximize total production and minimize cost. While "consultation" assures the systematic growth of science, the competitive forces at work in scientific life tend to bring about the most economic use both of the intellectual power and the material resources applied to the pursuit of discovery.

But something is yet missing in this analysis. The public discussion by which scientific claims are sifted before they can be accepted as established by science, is a process of mutual adjustment which is neither consultative nor competitive. This type of adjustment is exemplified by two opposing counsel trying to win over the jury to their own side. When such a discussion goes on in wider circles, each participant adjusts his arguments to what has been said before and thus all divergent and mutually exclusive aspects of a case are in turn revealed, the public being eventually persuaded to accept one (or some) and to reject the others. The persons participating in the controversy by which this result is achieved, may be said to co-operate in a system of spontaneous order. This type of co-ordination resembles a competitive order in view of the part played in it by the struggle of different individuals trying to achieve mutually exclusive advantages. But in a controversy that is both sincere and fair, the participants will primarily aim at presenting the truth, relying on it to prevail over error. Therefore, I suggest that co-ordination involved in a sincere and fair controversy should be classed separately as a system of *spontaneous order based on persuasion*. The mutual co-ordination of scientific activities is thus seen to include modes of interaction of all three kinds: consultation in the first place, competition as second in importance, and persuasion as third.

Law and science are only two among the many intellectual fields in society. Though no other activities of the mind form such precise systems as those of legal and scientific thought, they all prosper similarly by the mutually adjusted efforts of individual contributors. Thus language and writing are developed by individuals communicating through them with each other. Literature and the various arts, pictorial as well as musical; the crafts, including medicine, agriculture, manufacture and the various technical services; the whole body of religious, social and political thought—all these, and many other branches of human culture, are fostered by methods of spontaneous order similar to those described for science and law. Each of these fields represents a common heritage accessible to all, to which creative individuals in each successive generation respond in the form of proposed innovations, which, if accepted, are assimilated to the common heritage and passed on for the guidance of generations yet to come.

ACQUISITIVENESS VERSUS PROFESSIONALISM

Ever since its gradual rise in the Middle Ages, modern capitalism has been under fire of criticism, first by the Churches and then by the Socialist movement, for making profit-seeking the means for earning a living. R. H. Tawney who in his *Religion and the Rise of Capitalism* recorded the earlier stages of this criticism, contributed as a Socialist to its present phase in his book *The Acquisitive Society*. He expresses here the desire, which has always played some part in Socialist aspirations, that industrial life should be guided by professional standards, in place of the pursuit of personal gain.[4]

I have analysed, side by side, economic and intellectual systems of spontaneous order and have shown that the individual actions by which the former operate are purely

---

4. "The difference [writes Tawney] between industry as it exists to-day and a profession is then simple and unmistakable. . . . The essence of the one is that its only criterion is the financial return that it offers to its shareholders. The essence of the other is that, though men enter it for the sake of a livelihood, the measure of their success is the service which they perform not the gains which they amass." *The Acquisitive Society*, p. 108.

competitive, while those of the second are in the first place consultative, i.e. adjusted with reference to an established professional opinion. It is easy to see now why this must be so.

An intellectual system of spontaneous order can arise only within an existing system of thought. Such a system, transmitted by tradition, may absorb new entrants and guide their contributions in accordance with the traditional standards inherent in it. Systems of this kind may be in danger of exhaustion; they may be undermined by the growth of an internal contradiction or disrupted by dissension over some new issue. But so long as such a system lives and is believed true, its cultivation is recognized as a purpose in itself and its standards are accepted in their own right as guides to the cultivators' actions. Such a system of thought can in fact exist only when embodied in a social structure which is dedicated to the task of embodying it.

Economic activities cannot be guided by professional standards because there exists no system of thought from which such standards could be derived in respect to this field. It is foolish to look for standards of propriety which would rationally determine the distribution of such an immense variety of goods—millions of lines of merchandise— as a modern industrial system is expected to produce. The success of industrial production, undertaken to satisfy individual consumers' wants, must ultimately be tested by the consumers' satisfaction. And the only rational test of this, at least in the vast majority of cases, is the consumers' willingness to buy the product in a competitive market at a price which yields a profit to the makers. Producers therefore must seek to make a profit by selling their products and this profit must be their guide.

The reverse holds again for activities dedicated to the cultivation of a system of thought. For firstly, it is impossible to parcel up and hand out to individual consumers the results of such labours, which in fact cannot be consumed at all. The satisfaction which they give is of an inherently communal nature, as that given by beautiful public buildings or victories in war. And secondly, even if the results could somehow be individually consumed, the individual members of the public would not be competent to judge them, but would have to take their lead from the guardians of the professional standards who act as the public's agents in supervising the various fields of mental cultivation and supplying an authoritative assessment of their fruits.

FINANCING OF INTELLECTUAL ACTIVITIES

If intellectual products cannot in general be valued by what they fetch on the market, some other method must be applied for providing their makers with appropriate rewards and, where necessary, with laboratories and other resources of intellectual production. I have dealt with such questions before, in discussing the governmental financing of universities and have recommended there that in all particulars the public authorities should follow the guidance of professional opinion. It may be added here that the total sum of money allocated for cultural purposes will have to be assessed by the public authorities in relation to alternative modes of spending these sums, either by the individual citizens for their personal satisfaction, or by the public authorities for other collective purposes. Such decisions require of public opinion that it develop a sense of fitness, which can equally recognize extravagant spending and crying deficiencies in the cultural budget, and keep a rational middle course which will avoid both. This is the type of judgment on which the size and pattern of public or semi-public cultural expenditure is based. In earlier days it decreed the allocation of great wealth for the construction of cathedrals, parish churches, and monasteries, the bare maintenance of which has become precarious to-day, though they could rely for support on a much larger and richer population. Instead secular schools and universities are rapidly expanded to-day, particular munificence being lavished on the construction of laboratories. The totals—and ultimately of course also the various items—of these endowments are arrived at in each case by an assesment of marginal social returns, balanced against alternative marginal benefits, both social and individual.

Let us recall also an important intellectual activity, the fruits of which cannot be altogether assessed by professional opinion, but must primarily be valued by what they can fetch in the market. Inventions and other advances in technical knowledge resemble advances in pure science in that they benefit society best when enjoyed freely by all, but they differ from pure science in that they can be justified only by the test of profitability. It is interesting how difficult it is to devise institutions which will provide a commercial test for the profitability of inventions and yet leave the knowledge which they convey freely available to all.[5] Suppose that those who supply resources for the development of inventions wanted to collect their invested capital and any expected profits from the sale of the products made by the inventions. They would find this impossible, so long as the invention developed by them would become without delay available to everybody. For their competitors, getting the inventions free of charge, could—and probably would—undersell them, by the very amount required for recovering the cost of development. Hence the financing of inventions (it would seem) can be rationally conducted only if a legal title to the exclusive exploitation of inventions is

5. A detailed analysis of this subject is given in my paper "Patent Reform," *Review of Economic Studies,* 1944.

granted to those who financed them; but such a restriction is inappropriate to inventions as a form of knowledge and will greatly reduce their usefulness to society. Moreover, since it is impossible to define rationally the legal titles in question, the procedure for establishing the inventor's monopoly, which is that of the patent law, involves all the notorious injustices which abound in the operations of that law. There can hardly exist another institution which is so generally condemned as unsatisfactory among experts, while they seem to offer no hope whatever of an effective remedy for its shortcomings.

Part II

Formal Analysis

The impasse in which we find ourselves to-day in respect to the rational financing of inventions, offers a vivid example of a whole range of more momentous embarrassments. We see here an objective which we feel that society should be able to achieve and for the attainment of which no institution can be devised. It is an instance of a social task that for the time being we must consider as unmanageable.

The existence of social tasks which appear both desirable and feasible and yet are in fact impracticable has set the stage throughout history for a wide range of human conflicts. All the battles of social reform were fought on these grounds, with conservatives often harshly overstating and progressives recklessly underestimating the limits of manageability. There is hardly a social evil which was not authoritatively defended at some time or other as part of the natural order of things. Since the beginning of the last century social reform had regularly to face opponents who criticized its projects as contrary to the laws of political economy. Dickens wrote in *Hard Times* a revealing satire on the economic theories current among the manufacturers of Coketown:

> They were ruined when they were required to send children to school; they were ruined when inspectors were appointed to look into their works; they were ruined when such inspectors considered it doubtful whether they were quite justified in chopping up people with their machinery; they were utterly undone when it was hinted that perhaps they need not always make so much smoke.

Indeed, not more than fifteen years have passed since economic theory gave general support to the doctrine that periodic mass unemployment was ineradicable; a disastrous view which to-day few would accept. Yet the danger of disregarding the limits of social feasibility are no less terrible. Lenin's attempt to replace the functions of the market by a centrally directed economic system caused far greater devastation than the worst forms of *laissez-faire* ever did. There is no general method by which the two fateful opposite errors can be avoided. When history has been reviewed, we are still left with the responsibility for making up our minds on every new occasion as to what social objectives we should consider as attainable, and which as impossible. This is the problem of social manageability.

POLYCENTRICITY

In the present essay I have hitherto been concerned with extending the concept of self-co-ordination—known since Adam Smith to operate within a market—to various other activities in the intellectual field and with clarifying the relationship between the economic and intellectual systems thus brought into analogy to each other. I have shown before[6] that a task which is achieved spontaneously by mutual adjustment cannot be performed deliberately through a corporate body. Now I want to define certain social tasks which may or may not be manageable; but which, if manageable, can only be performed by spontaneous mutual adjustment. I shall pursue this aim by enlarging upon the concept of *polycentricity*. This concept can be defined by the use of the models shown in Figures 1 and 2.

A framework built of rods is shown in Figure 1. We see six pin-points at the edge, each of which is connected with every other by a rod or a tie or strut. Now suppose we hang

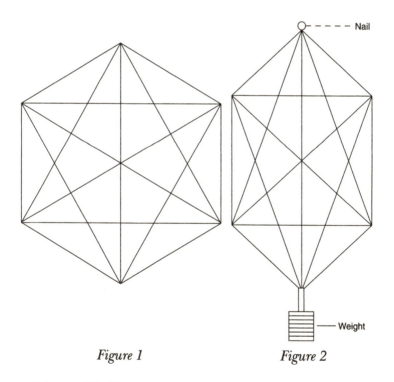

Figure 1   *Figure 2*

6. See pp. 141–49.

this framework up by one pin-point to a nail and attach a heavy weight to the pin-point just opposite, as shown in Figure 2. The whole structure will be distorted in a definite manner, each pin-point being displaced in respect to every other. To calculate the ensuing lengthenings and shortenings of the rods we have to know their elastic properties, i.e. the lengthening or shortening that each would undergo under a given pull or push acting along its axis. Armed with such knowledge we could set up a number of simultaneous equations, which would state that the strains imposed on the rods connecting one pin-point with the rest are such as to produce a resultant force equal to zero at every pin-point, excepting the two at which the framework is loaded and at which it is attached to the nail, where the resultant should be equal and opposite to the loads acting on the pin-points.[7]

The mutual displacement of the pin-points in the loaded framework possesses "polycentricity," i.e. the pin-points are so displaced that the displacement of each in respect to every other is related in a prescribed manner to the displacement of every one of these to each of the others— and so on indefinitely. I shall say that the totality of these displacements represents a case of *polycentric order.* The task of ordering a number of elements polycentrically will be called a *polycentric task.*

The loaded framework illustrates a polycentric task of a particular kind, namely one that can be mathematically *formalized.* Its performance can be given the form of solving a set of simultaneous equations. This is due to the fact that the relations (i.e. displacements) requiring adjustment between the individual centres can be *specified* in the form of

7. The unloaded framework is assumed to be free of internal strain, and the weight of the rods is assumed to be negligible; their connection at the corners leaves them to swing around freely in the plane of the figure.

numerically measured quantities, fulfilling specifiable equations. Polycentric tasks which can be mathematically formalized fall into three groups. Some can be computed *exactly*, others only *by a sequence of successive approximations*, and others again are altogether *incomputable*.

By an exact computation I mean one which simultaneously takes into account all the conditions of the task and operates methodically on the symbols representing them, until the unknown arrangement determined by the known conditions of the problem is brought out as an explicit function of these conditions. Exact computations can only be carried out for polycentric tasks involving a comparatively small number of centres. The number is subject to two kinds of limitations. One limitation arises from the limited accuracy of the experimental data that enter into the calculation. The "elastic properties" of rods are always known only to a limited degree of accuracy (at the best to about 1 per cent.) and when these magnitudes are introduced into the formulae for the unknown displacements, their inaccuracies usually have a cumulative effect on the result which rapidly mounts up with the number of centres involved. It is on this account—it would seem—that R. V. Southwell expresses this fact when stating in his *Theory of Elasticity* (1935, p. 111), that the greatest number of simultaneous linear equations representing a loaded framework, which could be treated with any confidence in the accuracy of the final result, was ten or twelve.[8] There exists, however, another limitation which arises even if the "given data" entering into the set of simultaneous equations are supposed to be known with absolute accuracy. This is due, as J. v. Neumann and H. H. Goldstine have shown[9] to

8. This point was confirmed by correspondence with Sir Richard Southwell.

9. *Bull. Amer. Math. Soc.*, 53 (1947), 1021.

the fact that you have to "round off" the numbers obtained in the course of calculating the unknowns in an extensive set of linear equations. Calculations of this kind are impracticable unless carried out with the help of computing machines, and these can handle only a limited number of digits. v. Neumann and Goldstine have estimated that the number (k) of simultaneous linear equations that can be evaluated by any modern computing machine would be limited to 150. This restriction $(k < 150)$ is derived for a machine handling twelve decimal or forty binary digits. The former, it so happens, is the digital range of ordinary desk calculating machines, the latter that of the modern electronic computer. The limitations imposed on k on account of the "rounding off" error are therefore the same in both cases. But the desk machine reaches its effective limit at a much lower k, on account of its low speed. For the evaluation of k equations requires about k^3 multiplications, which with $k = 150$ is about 3,500,000; and even for the electronic computer, this would require in practice (according to an estimate for which I am indebted to Professor M. H. A. Newman) a time of about ten hours. While the "rounding off" error could be reduced in electronic computers without excessive difficulty by increasing the number of digits handled, its speed limit makes an extension of its range beyond $k = 150$ appear impracticable. It may be mentioned that we assumed here throughout that we are concerned with systems of equations in which practically all the co-efficients of the unknown quantities have significant values. A framework of the kind shown in Figure 1 with suitable loads attached to it, should represent a problem possessing this quality.

The upshot of this discussion is to set a limit on the number of corners n which our polygonal framework can have if its distortion under load is to be numerically computable. There is a formula for k, (the order of redundancy), according to which $k = r - 2j + 3$, with $r =$ number of rods and $j =$ number of joints. In our case

$$j = n \text{ and } r = \frac{n(n-1)}{2},$$

and hence $k = 150$ is first reached for about $n = 20$. We conclude that the polycentric task represented by the distortion under load of an n-cornered polygon of the type shown in Figure 1 can be computed by exact methods (in the sense defined above) only up to the limit of $n = 20$.

A wide range of formalized polycentric problems of which the solutions lie beyond the power of exact calculation can be solved by a suitable method of approximation, which is of great interest to us as it represents a perfect paradigm of a co-ordination by independent mutual adjustments. The method consists in dealing with *one centre at a time while supposing the others to be fixed in relation to the rest, for that time.*[10] This procedure is called the "relaxation method," which R. V. Southwell developed systematically and brought to prominence in the science of engineering in 1935.[11] You deal with each centre by calculating its displacement in respect to the others which are assumed to remain fixed. By performing this "adjustment" for each centre in turn, you obtain a first—perhaps rather crude—approximation to the required polycentric order. By repeating the "adjustment" of each centre, the correct shape of the loaded framework can be approximated to any desired extent. It will usually suffice to go over all centres two or three times.

10. A passing reference has already been made to this on p. 175 above.

11. See R. V. Southwell, *Theory of Elasticity* (1935), and in more detail in *Relaxation Methods in Engineering Science* (1940), and *Relaxation Methods in Theoretical Physics* (1946).

The Relaxation Method presupposes that the problem of every single centre can be computed by exact methods. This permits the indefinite extension of a polycentric task, so long as the extension involves no increase in the difficulty of the computation to be made at each centre. This is usually true; it holds for example for large frameworks used in railway bridges or aeroplanes, where the number of braces pinned together at each joint does not increase with the size of the framework. But if in a fully braced polygon (i.e. one in which each corner is connected with every other corner) the number of centres is increased, the problem at each centre becomes increasingly more difficult and at some stage the problem becomes altogether incomputable. For the problem of "adjusting" one corner of a fully braced polygon (in which case $j = 1$) we find that the limit $k = 150$ will be reached when $n = 153$. Between $n = 20$ and $n = 153$ we can therefore evaluate the problems of fully braced loaded polygons by the aid of successive approximations from corner to corner; while beyond that (i.e. for $n > 153$) lies a region in which computation is no longer possible at all.

The analogy between the operation of the Relaxation Method and a series of mutual adjustments leading to a system of spontaneous order, can be made even more striking by the following imaginary procedure. For the numerical evaluation of a very urgent polycentric problem, we could employ a team of mathematicians of whom each would be put in charge of one centre. He would be instructed to carry out the adjustment of his centre and to announce the result to all the other calculators. Once each had noted the result of all the others he would make a second adjustment of his own centre, which would take into account the adjustments previously made by all the others at theirs. Thus in a few consecutive steps a polycentric task of any size could be carried out at the same high speed, provided only that the problems arising at the individual centres remained of the same degree of difficulty.

We have here a replica of the team of jig-saw puzzle solvers described earlier on to illustrate the logic of self-co-ordination among scientists.[12] Our new paradigm, however, is in various ways an advance on the earlier version. The team of calculators who most effectively combine to achieve their polycentric task by operating independently at each centre, is not a fiction but represents the actual process by which engineering science masters its polycentric problems. The superiority of the Relaxation Method, on which our model of spontaneous order is based, is notorious; its practical value in solving otherwise insoluble problems is well established. Moreover, the exact method of computing polycentric problems, the range of which appears so limited by comparison, supplies us—as a counter-part to self-co-ordination—with a model of co-ordination by one central authority. The exact method of computing a set of simultaneous equations takes note simultaneously of all the conditions to which the several centres of the problem are subject and finally produces an adjustment of each in which all these conditions (expressed by the whole array of co-efficients) simultaneously enter. This is precisely what a central co-ordinating authority would have to do, and the comparative impotence of this procedure is a true illustration of the impotence of central direction as compared with a process of mutual self-adjustment.

The team of polycentric calculators has a further advantage in illustrating spontaneous co-ordination in society. It establishes the kind of order which individuals operating in the same market establish between themselves. The polycentric task achieved by the calculators is a minimum problem, and

12. P. 43 above.

the task aimed at by the market can be described in similar terms: market operations tend towards a minimum of costs and a maximum of satisfaction, which has been jointly described as a maximum of economic utility.

But before evaluating this parallel we must extend our conception of polycentric tasks. Hitherto I have talked only of polycentric problems that can be mathematically formulated, such as are commonly presented to the engineer and also occur all over the field of science, for example as the many-body problems of astronomy and atomic physics. In a wider sense, however, we may consider every problem of balancing a large number of elements as a polycentric task. The system of postural reflexes which keep us in equilibrium while sitting, standing or walking, performs a very complex polycentric task. And from this purely animal level we may ascend continuously to the highest intellectual, moral and artistic achievements. Wisdom is defined by Kant as a man's capacity to harmonize all his purposes in life; thus wisdom aims at a polycentric task. In a painting each patch of colour should bear a significant relation to every other patch. Mozart is quoted as saying that he could simultaneously hear all the notes of an opera which he had just finished composing. All art aims at polycentric harmonies. Between the reflex reactions and the supremely creative levels there are many intermediate levels of practical intelligence, which raise similar many-sided problems. A well-assorted menu will combine dishes and wines harmoniously and a wise gastronomer will adjust his helpings of each so as to make the most of all. A doctor will prescribe a cure for a trouble of the lungs, while considering also the heart, the kidneys and the digestion as well as the income and the family conditions of the patient. All these are polycentric tasks which cannot be mathematically formulated.

The solving of polycentric tasks of this kind is a characteristic ability of living beings and of animals in particular.
On the lowest levels it may be identified with the capacity
for homoeostasis or purposive action, while its higher forms
manifest man's power of intelligent judgment. In either
case the balance is achieved by an organism reacting to the
whole range of impulses that reach it from all the "centres"
which it jointly takes into account. The organism evaluates
their joint significance, whether reflexly or consciously, and,
thus guided, produces a solution of the polycentric task, or
achieves, at any rate, a measure of success in this direction.

Between such polycentric tasks which are *completely un-
formalized* and those of the engineer which are *completely formalized,* there is an intermediate range of tasks which I shall
describe as *"theoretically formalized."*

Economic tasks fall into this class. In a wider sense all
polycentric tasks are economic, for it is of the essence of all
problems to be set within certain limiting conditions and a
polycentric task always aims at making the best within these
limits of a number of elements available for a joint purpose.
But a problem becomes more narrowly economic if the numerous "elements" are different kinds of consumable goods
or different forms of resources applied to the production of
these goods, and the limitation consists in the scarcity of
these resources and of the goods produced from them. The
particular kind of wisdom, or prudence, required to deal with
such situations is called "economy" in the technical sense.

First among its oft-described exemplars is the prudent
housewife, spreading her expenditure over all possible purchases so as to maximize their total utility. Each item she
spends should be balanced against every other item, this in
turn being balanced against every other, and so on indefinitely. This is the polycentric task of the consumer's choice.
Robinson Crusoe has an even more complex polycentric

task to solve if he wishes to balance every item of the simple needs and pleasures which he satisfies, both against each other and against every item of effort expended on gaining these satisfactions—while each effort in its turn would have to be balanced against every other effort and against each form of satisfaction to which it contributes. This defines the polycentric task of self-subsistent production.

The judgment exercised by the shopping housewife or the self-subsistent farmer in carrying out their tasks has certain features which make it suitable for mathematical formulation, which it would be useless to attempt for other fields of prudence or to artistic decisions. The goods which are consumed and the labour expended can be specified quantitatively, or may at any rate be supposed to be so specifiable, without serious distortion of the facts. This has stimulated the setting up of mathematical equations illustrating the problems facing the housewife and the self-subsistent producer. The significance of these equations is, however, quite different from that of the mathematically expressed problems of engineering or astronomy, which I have described as fully formalized. For, firstly—and obviously—housewives and farmers know nothing about the equations which are supposed to set out their problems, nor would they understand them if they knew about them. And secondly, these equations cannot be evaluated, for the substitution-coefficients which enter into them cannot be measured and the symbols referring to these are therefore without numerical significance. These equations are valuable in exhibiting certain logical features of the problem to which they refer, but cannot be used for solving these problems. They offer a mathematical model of economic decisions. If the consumer could be represented by a robot,[13] the function of

13. See p. 173 above.

the robot could be fully specified in mathematical terms and these would satisfy equations of the kind by which economic theory describes the consumer's problem. Similarly, a mechanical Robinson Crusoe would have to satisfy the mathematical theory of the self-subsistent producer. It is in this sense that I said that the economic problems to which I have referred are *theoretically formalizable.* Their mathematical formulation is significant only in theory, not in practice.

I should mention here that the economic problem facing industrial managers can also be theoretically formalized. It consists in the maximization of profits by transforming productive resources into articles that can be sold, particularly to consumers, both the resources and the products being valued at given current prices. The mathematical formulation of managerial functions is, once more, merely a mathematical model. A modern industrial manager will use more computations (directly or indirectly) than Robinson Crusoe, but most of the "data" on which he relies can obviously not be given numerical values, or brought into mathematically specifiable relations to each other.

The major result of economic theory is to show that an aggregate of individuals, solving as Producers and Consumers the problems theoretically assigned to them, would achieve self-co-ordination as if directed by an "invisible hand." The resulting system of spontaneous order is defined as a minimum of production costs, combined with a maximum utility of distribution. A long list of qualifications ought to be added to this statement to make it quite clear that the minimum of costs is a *relative minimum,* which would vary according to the institutional framework, e.g. for every stage of social legislation—and that the maximum of utility is a *relative maximum,* defined with respect to a certain distribution of incomes, a certain level of honesty among salesmen and credulity among customers, and so on and so forth. While all these qualifications must be remembered, they should never be allowed to obscure the fact that some *relative* optimum is achieved according to economic theory by independent economic actions of a multitude of individuals, acting both as "Producers" and "Consumers."

The economic optimum achieved by the invisible hand in society can now be compared with the minimum problem evaluated by our team of calculators, adjusting a polycentric framework to a given set of loads. The solution which the computers will find is characterized by a minimum value of the stress-energy stored in the rods of the framework carrying the given loads. Similarly, the individuals solving their several economic problems within the same market, evaluate by their independent mutual adjustments the polycentric task of optimum allocation of resources and distribution of products. In either case, the overall problem can be represented by a set of simultaneous linear equations. This will actually determine the solution for the framework, while supplying only a theoretical model of the economic problem of society.[14] The calculators carry out an actual mathematical operation, while the individuals in economic life solve the several problems by a comprehensive judgment which can be formalized only in theory. We may note also that the problems of the computers are not polycentric and must be solved rigorously, while the mathematical model representing the economic problems of "Producers" and "Consumers" is always polycentric.

14. The first comprehensive mathematical formulation of this problem is due to Enrico Barone (1908) whose paper on "The Ministry of Production in the Collectivist State," followed up an earlier suggestion of Pareto in *Cours d'economie politique,* II, 1897. Barone's paper was reprinted in English as an Appendix to *Collectivist Economic Planning,* ed. F. A. Hayek, Routledge, (1935).

MANAGEABILITY OF SOCIAL TASKS

We can now resume our examination of manageability and (even at the risk of some repetitions) state more systematically the results to be derived for the limits of manageability from the concept of polycentricity.

In order to give precision to the notion of manageability we should characterize tasks without regard to the manner of their actual performance and indeed—irrespective of the fact whether they can be performed at all. Only then could we undertake to survey the field of conceivable tasks, select those that are manageable and decide by what means each could be carried out. This programme, however, seems too vast for practical purposes, as it would demand the formulation of an indefinite range of impossible tasks. It is preferable, therefore, to approach the matter in a piecemeal manner by examining some of the tasks that are normally performed to-day and the methods which are successful in achieving them. Once it is clear why certain tasks can be performed in a certain manner, we can explore rationally a limited field of unmanageable tasks bordering on those that are manageable. We may thus define a frontier beyond which lie tasks which for the time being must be pronounced *unmanageable*—as well as, no doubt, the tasks which the future progress of thought may yet teach us to master.

Polycentricity, as defined by the loaded framework in Figure 2, was introduced in order to characterize certain tasks, which having been thus defined, were divided into three kinds: (1) formalizable, (2) not formalizable, (3) theoretically formalizable. Only a small range of comparatively simple formalizable polycentric problems can be evaluated exactly: i.e. by taking into account simultaneously all the conditions of the problem. However far the improvement of computational methods may extend that range, there will always lie beyond it a vastly greater range of more complex polycentric problems which can be solved only by approximation from centre to centre. This method can be effectively organized and speeded up by using a team of independent calculators, one for each centre. The proper method of managing a polycentric task is therefore not by collecting all the data at one centre and evaluating them jointly. The much more powerful and more accurate method is to solve the problem in respect to one centre at a time, while pretending blindness in respect to all other conditions set by the problem as a whole, that is to the overwhelming majority of the relations to be fulfilled. It is the "unplanned" activity of a team of independent calculators each of whom limits his interest to the single centre of which he is in charge, which thus appears to be supported by the authority of established scientific practice.

Only when a task can be formalized as a mathematical problem can it be rigorously defined, irrespective of the way it may be carried out. You have not clearly decided on decorating a wall by a mural painting or on having a statue erected, until you have chosen the artist to do it. If instead of commissioning one artist to paint your portrait, you decide to have it done by a committee of painters, whose members should take turns at applying the brush to the canvas, you will undoubtedly get something that is a painting, but it will clearly be very different from what an individual artist could have accomplished. These examples illustrate that task and performance cannot be kept well apart in the case of non-formalizable problems.

I have explained that economic problems take up an intermediate position between fully formalizable and entirely unformalizable tasks: they are *theoretically* formalizable. We can set up mathematical models of economic problems and speculate on mathematical methods of solving them. The fact that a mathematical model can be set up of the functions performed by a market economy as a whole, has in the past lent strength to the idea that the economic system could be managed centrally by solving the set of simultaneous equations constituting this model.[15] This project has been opposed by F. A. Hayek[16] on the grounds of its twofold impracticability; that it would be impossible to collect the requisite numerical data and that even if these were made available, the task of carrying out the proposed computations would be excessive.

The foregoing discussion of polycentricity goes somewhat further in clarifying the situation. It points out firstly, that a theoretical model which is useful in revealing the system of choices involved in the economic system cannot in fact be used for calculating the result of these choices, because the symbols representing the "given data" have mostly no numerical significance. It does not essentially matter for this conclusion if the argument is restricted to the mathematical evaluation of only part of the choices performed in the economic system, as it is in the writings of the authors I have quoted above. Managerial skill can as little be replaced by a mathematical computation than housewifely prudence or a worker's preference of one job for another when seeking employment. To assume empirically established "demand curves" for individually consumed products and similarly observed "supply curves" for productive resources, does not elevate therefore

15. H. D. Dickinson, "Price Formation in a Socialist Community," *Economic Journal* (1933). In O. Lange and F. M. Taylor, *On the Economic Theory of Socialism* (1938), and H. D. Dickinson, *Economics of Socialism* (1939), the solving of the simultaneous equations is still contemplated, but other methods of management are preferred. However, more recently Th. Balogh, (*Political Quarterly*, 1944, p. 258) refers to Barone as having indicated—by the mathematical formulation of the economic optimum—the principles of a centrally planned economy.

16. F. A. Hayek in *Collectivist Economic Planning*, London (1935).

the simultaneous equations defining the problem of production beyond the status of a mathematical model.

Secondly, the much-vexed question as to the amount and worthwhileness of labour involved in evaluating a large set of simultaneous equations (H. D. Dickinson[17] mentions sets of two or three thousand) has to be reconsidered in the light of what has been said concerning the computability of such sets. The number of simultaneous equations that can be successfully computed is usually restricted to very few indeed, on account of the inaccuracy of the given data. If your results tend to become meaningless in a problem of elastic deformation if you choose cases represented by more than twelve simultaneous equations, it is not likely that you will have many instances of economic equilibria with sufficiently accurately given data to justify larger systems of equations.[18] Moreover, it is difficult to see how the amount of labour which we are prepared to devote to the evaluation of such a system can materially shift the limit of $k < 150$, since

17. *Economics of Socialism,* p. 104.

18. (*a*) Provided of course that all the data have significant values; if their vast majority is zero, the problem degenerates and can no longer be treated within the framework of this argument.

(*b*) Economic calculations based on as much as fifty simultaneous linear equations have been recently carried out by Professor Wassily Leontief in evaluating "input-output" relations. I have been unable to find any published discussion of the effect which the inaccuracies of the given data had on the significance of his final results. An emphatic warning was given in this respect by Professor Oscar Morgenstern in a discussion of Professor Leontief's paper to the American Economic Association (Cleveland, Ohio, Dec. 27–30, 1948) published in the *American Economic Review,* 39, 1949, p. 238. While Morgenstern admits that "the solution of simultaneous linear equations of numbers exceeding twenty or thirty is not an impossible undertaking to-day" he clearly indicates that this can be done only "by gathering data of superior quality with the errors of observation known as much as possible."

e.g., a tenfold increase of this limit would increase the time of computation about a thousandfold, and extend it over a whole year of continuous labour. By that time all the data would have become obsolete.

Even if both these points could be overcome we know now that the proper way of evaluating the polycentric problem represented by the equations of an economic optimum would not consist in the direct evaluation of this set of equations, but in a process of approximation from centre to centre. The lesson of the Relaxation Method is that this procedure affords an enormous gain in speed, precision and economy of effort, and may be regarded in general as the only feasible one.[19] It teaches us that, contrary to the usual view, the true scientific handling of an economic system of many centres does not consist in taking into account jointly all the elements of the problem, but in disregarding their vast majority at each move, exactly in the way in which a system of profit-seeking individuals in fact operates in a market of resources and products.

I should like, however, to re-state these conclusions once more quite apart from the controversy about central planning. *Just as a set of simultaneous equations represents the mathematical model of a polycentric system of economy, so the Relaxation Method represents the mathematical model of the manner in which economic operations carried out independently at each economic centre, produce the solution of the economic task.* Overall self-co-ordination of the activities performed at each economic centre results from the same logic as for the team of calculators described before. The scope of evaluation by self-co-

---

19. Suppose you have 1,000 computing machines operating at a thousand centres of one polycentric task and that you could replace these by one single machine evaluating the whole problem; the amount of labour would be increased a millionfold.

ordination is vastly greater than that of evaluation by central direction; it will succeed over a wide range of polycentricity in which central direction is completely impracticable. In making use of these conclusions it should always be borne in mind that they are merely an amplification of a mathematical model which cannot be actually evaluated, for most of the symbols representing the "given data" have no numerical significance. The evaluation of the local problems arising at each economic centre is in fact done by a balanced assessment of the situation at that centre, without any calculation at all.

The conclusions drawn here from the polycentric nature of the economic task are more general than those reached in the preceding essay, *The Span of Central Direction* (p. 136 above). I started there from the assumption that the market does in fact produce a system of spontaneous order and thus solves—as we would now say—a polycentric task. It was then shown that this form of social management could not be replaced by that of corporate order, without paralysing the execution of the polycentric task. Beyond this, no attempt was made there at examining the justification of the market as a method of overall economic management.

Part III

Critique of Freedom

THE GOVERNMENT OF SPONTANEOUS ORDER

Having sufficiently emphasized the qualifications to which it is subject, we shall carry forward for further discussion the following thesis: "A polycentric task can be socially managed only by a system of mutual adjustments."

From this it immediately follows that if no system of mutual adjustments can be devised which will lead to the social performance of a polycentric task, then it is socially unmanageable. In other words, such a task can be approximated only to the extent to which a system of feasible mutual adjustments will lead to something resembling it. The implications of this conclusion will be more easily recognized if we first cast a brief glance at the institutions which uphold mutual adjustment in the existing systems of spontaneous order.

In an earlier part of this book I have described broadly the institutions through which scientific opinion rules over scientific life and maintains vital contacts with circles outside science. All intellectual systems of spontaneous order are similarly governed by professional opinion, which is usually organized into a professional body.

Spontaneous economic systems are not governed by professional opinion, for which sufficient foundation is lacking, but by institutions of property and exchange. Dominant over these is the code of private law. In the Code Civil of France (leaving out of account the law of the family) Duguit finds only three fundamental rules and no more—freedom of contract, the inviolability of property, and the duty to compensate another for damage due to one's own fault.[20] Thus it transpires that the main function of the existing spontaneous order of jurisdiction is to govern the spontaneous order of economic life. A *consultative* system of law develops and enforces the rules under which the *competitive* system of production and distribution operates. No marketing system can function without a legal framework which guarantees adequate proprietary powers and enforces contracts.

20. J. Walter Jones, *Historical Introduction to the Theory of Law,* Oxford (1940) p. 114.

The greatest difficulty in a system of universal State ownership of industry, as now established in Soviet Russia and approximated in the countries adjoining Russia, lies in the absence of an effective legal order which would enforce contracts and allocate responsibility for damages according to fixed rules. There exists a complete Civil Code in Russia proper which could be called upon for this purpose.[21] Time and again the Soviet Government has pressed its enterprises to fight for their rights against each other, realizing that only in this manner could order be maintained within its productive system. Yet these appeals do not seem to have taken effect. All Soviet enterprises are financed and strictly controlled by various branches of the same State Bank, to which they have to account for their funds. Further control over these enterprises is exercised by the central planning authority, which supervises their output. Considering these tight restrictions as well as the state of chronic inflation which makes all goods saleable without serious losses, it is not surprising that Soviet enterprises show no initiative or inclination to go to court against each other, in order to secure payment from a defaulting contractual partner. Thus the fitful and sporadic fulfilment of contractual obligations in Russia continues to spread disorder and confirms that the existence and application of private law is an essential requirement for the maintenance of an ordered polycentric system of production, even under universal State ownership.

21. "Soviet Russia has now a full set of Codes and Acts such as usually compose the private or commercial legislation of a modern country," writes S. Dobrin in the *Law Quarterly Review,* Vol. 49 (1933) p. 260. "Here and there [he says] a bourgeois lawyer may find in a Soviet Commercial Act some clause or clauses reminding him that the act which he has in his hands is an act of a socialist State, but the bulk of the act will appear to him extremely familiar—more or less an ordinary enactment of an ordinary modern country on the matter in question."

MANAGEABILITY OF SOCIAL TASKS

Generally speaking, the mutual adjustments required for the establishment of a competitive economic order must be initiated by individual agents empowered to dispose of resources and products, subject to general rules; these mutual adjustments are bargains concluded through the market; the application of general rules to conflicts between bargainers constitutes the legal order of private law, which is itself a system of mutual adjustments. Economic liberty and an important range of juridical independence thus jointly form the institutional basis for the social performance of an economic task of a polycentric character.

FREEDOM AND MANAGEABILITY

We have come to the conclusion that the social management of polycentric tasks requires a set of free institutions. More particularly, that the task of allocating a multitude of resources to a large number of productive centres for the purpose of processing them into products of such variety as is usual to-day and distributing the latter rationally to consumers numbering tens of millions, requires for its social management a system of civil law which establishes rights of (marketable) property and enforces contracts. This result is fairly close to what Marx expressed by saying that "the forces of production" determine "the relations of production." Had his followers correctly applied this view to the prospects of a system of state-ownership, they would have concluded that since this system had the same economic task to perform as capitalism, it could function only insofar as it operated through the same "productive relation," i.e. the same legal order of property and contract. That might have saved humanity from much useless strife.

The opposite error, committed by the adherents of *laissez-faire*, consisted essentially in assuming that there is only one economic optimum that can be achieved by the market and that, correspondingly, only one set of proprietary and contractual laws is compatible with an economy aiming at this unique economic optimum. I have quoted Dickens for a denunciation of the manner in which the evil effects of existing institutions were pronounced ineradicable by powerful interests, informed by popular economic theories, a hundred years ago. But it is fair to add that in spite of this the past century offered in practice a consistent denial of *laissez-faire*. It was the century of continuous social reform, which proved that there exists an indefinite range of relative optima towards which a market economy can tend. It demonstrated that it is the task of social legislation to discover and implement improvements of the institutional framework, for the purpose of deliberately modifying the system of spontaneous order established by the market.

This movement for economic reform may yet go on indefinitely. It largely embodies our hopes of a good society. But there is a considerable literature to-day which displays much ingenuity in suggesting improvements of the economic optimum, while hardly paying any attention to the question of their institutional implementation. The theoretical formalization of economic tasks lends us the power to define precisely a whole range of such tasks, quite irrespective of their manageability. Modern economic theory has provided us with a valuable analysis of the limitations to which the existing system of private enterprise is subject, such as imperfect competition, increasing returns and indivisible cost-items; and this has led to the formulation of new systems in which these shortcomings are eliminated. Proposals were made for establishing perfect competition by replacing the test of commercial profit by the criterion that "marginal costs" be equated to "marginal returns." Other proposals included the governmental rewarding of investments yielding "increasing returns," on the basis of their total cost-curve. Under these new rules the market should tend towards perfect optima.

Most of the writers putting forward such suggestions were Socialists and implied that the new perfectioned market economy could be enforced under government ownership. But this neglects the problem of manageability. The fact that the State owns the shares of an enterprise and appoints its manager does not in itself lend it new powers of control over the manager. It could gain such powers only by inventing new tests of efficiency, which would work as reliably as those hitherto used by the private shareholders and yet impel the manager to do something different from what he did before. If, however, such tests could be invented and applied for rewarding fairly and consistently ten thousand state-appointed managers, the same tests could be equally applied for rewarding privately appointed managers and through them the shareholders of the enterprises. If they cannot be used for the control of private enterprises, neither can they be used for the control of public enterprises, for the problem of management involved in the two cases is the same.[22] Proposals for the perfectioning of the economic optimum to be achieved by the market, which disregard these institutional problems, are no more than exercises in the construction of mathematical models.

Some writers turn from the shortcomings of our marketing system to something vaguely designated as "the totalitarian alternative." Whether this is done in hope, fear or despair, it is in any case meaningless. Whatever the exact manner in which the economic system of totalitarian coun-

22. Compare pp. 184–88 above. See also A. W. Lewis, *Principles of Economic Planning*, 1949 (p. 104): "Nationalized industries must pay their way on a non-discriminatory basis."

tries operates—of which our information is still very incomplete—it is certainly not by direction from one centre. Most of the rigid economic controls exercised by the government (so far as they are genuine and not merely serving the presence of central planning) are concerned with the hemming in of an excessive monetary circulation.[23] There is no indication whatever in such facts as are known—as there is no possibility for it in theory—that totalitarian governments can establish a perfect economic optimum by exercising their legally unlimited executive powers.

Contemporary opinion with its indiscriminate taste for the explanation of historic events as rational responses to economic or technical requirements, is inclined to regard the abolition of economic and other freedom in Russia as an outcome of a "capitalist crisis" or of "modern technology," of the "necessity of rapid industrialization," and the like. These explanations, which have never been argued in detail, appear to be without any foundation, and do not in my view deserve the labour of refutation.

The "totalitarian alternative" is a figment of the mind, but there exist important alternatives on a smaller scale between different forms of management, corresponding to somewhat different economic tasks. If you want to keep unemployment down to one and a half per cent. as it is in Britain to-day, then you must put up (so long as the mobility of labour and capital is not greatly increased beyond its present level) with price controls, resulting in queueing of customers and their exposure to favouritism and discourtesy on the part of the shopkeepers, and put up also with a labyrinth of licensing laws which compel you for example to argue with an official whether you need a new bath-tub or not in place of one which shows depressing signs of half a

23. Compare p. 168 above.

century's use by past owners. Equalitarianism raises the same issues by contributing to inflationary pressure and produces, moreover, an unpleasant tendency towards improvident spending on business accounts. Again, in administering large-scale social services you may have to choose the degree to which you will check abuses by penalizing the most needy beneficiaries. Marginal choices between economic efficiency and economic liberty are real and important, and they form merely one instance among many similar choices between different kinds of social good that reformers must bear in mind at every turn.

To sum up so far the argument of this section. The economic optimum pursued by modern society to-day fundamentally determines the nature of the institutions required for its management; but this leaves open an unlimited possibility for creative reforms and even permits, though only over a narrow range, the joint variation of economic targets and of the institutions required for their achievement.

With this perspective in mind we may now return to the disturbing conclusion reached at the close of the preceding section, where I said that both economic liberty and judicial order established for safeguarding and governing economic liberty are justifiable only for the purpose of managing a particular economic task. If that is accepted, then (in spite of all the cautioning just given both against rigid and extremist assumptions) it follows that if the economic optimum at which we are aiming were radically changed, there might well be no place left either for economic liberty or for a system of contractual law within which to exercise that liberty, nor for a judicial system through which to develop and administer such law.

I believe this to be true, and there are a variety of cases which can be brought up to illustrate it. In the previous essay, *Profits and Polycentricity*, I have pointed out some relevant instances. If a modern economic system, once adjusted through the market, could go on operating indefinitely on identical lines of production and distribution, it would cease to represent a task of polycentric adjustments and could henceforth appropriately be governed by custom and public law. Assuming a stationary population, all productive functions could be made hereditary and the distributive system also fixed by a system of hereditary dues. We would have an economy based on status in which "the channels of social obligations function as substitute for the market." This quotation is from Raymond Firth's description of Polynesian economy.[24]

In an earlier essay, *The Span of Central Direction,* I have also mentioned the opposite extreme of an economy, subjected to technical changes of such rapidity that the re-allocation of resources and re-distribution of products cannot be left to the market, for fear of excessive windfall profits on the one hand and of quite undeserved hardships on the other. Such conditions arise regularly in wartime and call for rationing and price-control. These measures are again an attempt at replacing market-operations—at least partly—by a system of public law.

It is indeed quite easy, and not without interest, to construct examples of polycentric economic tasks which would

24. Raymond Firth, *Primitive Polynesian Economy* (1939), p. 36. The author seems to suggest that this form of economic management is unrelated to the economic task performed. "It must be emphasized [he says] that it is not the fewness of the native wants that allows the system to function without a price mechanism; it is the specific social pattern of the ways in which these wants are met, and the goods and service transferred." It may be that the economic function performed here—or something equivalent to it—could be carried out through the market, but the relevant point is that it would be totally impossible to establish a specific social pattern of personal obligations which would replace the usual functions of modern markets, while the fewness and the repetitive nature of the wants to be met in a primitive society permits to dispense with the market.

be entirely unmanageable by use of a market mechanism. I shall mention two of these.

(1) Assume the technology of production to be the same as it is at present: requiring the allocation of a large variety of resources to say a hundred thousand different productive centres; and add the condition that all products are either for collective use or are distributed in the form of gratuitous social services. The position is reached if we assume that taxation is increased (from forty per cent. as it averages to-day in Britain) to a hundred per cent. of income. There would then be no material incentives in earning wages, profits, etc., and no likelihood that men as producers would be prepared to compete for such payments if they were offered to them. In that case the polycentric task of producing at minimum costs (and of deciding a total level of production at which marginal costs would equal marginal product) would be strictly insoluble.[25]

(2) As a complementary example we may imagine a technology producing goods for the satisfaction of individual consumers, which does so mainly at the expense of social costs, i.e. smells, radiations, infections, noises, river-pollutions, general ugliness, etc., spreading all over the country; each factory causing a particular kind of social cost, which would depend in some definite manner on its output. The economic task of the community would then be to obtain a total of goods and services at a minimum of total social costs, expressed as a total of unpleasant repercussions, and to fix total output at a level where any further increase of these repercussions would be just equal and opposite to the marginal value of the total product. This is

25. Colin Clark, *Econ. Journ.*, 55 (1945), 371, has suggested that 25 per cent. of the national income may be about the limit for taxation in any non-totalitarian country in times of peace.

a polycentric task, since it requires the balancing of a large number of variable items against all others. We may exclude the possibility that the balance can be achieved within one mind and consequently its attainment would have to rely on a system of mutual adjustments between a large number of centres. This could be done if the nuisance created by each factory could be assessed as a function of its output and brought home to the manager in the form of fines, graded according to the output. But this is impossible, for there can exist no market for the mutual exchange of a great variety of smells, noises, infections, river-pollutions, etc., arising at thousands of different places. A technology of this kind would therefore be entirely unmanageable.

I shall concentrate for the purpose of the following argument on case 1. For it is quite within the realm of possibility that we might sometimes be forced to aim at an economic task of this kind. A wealthy country engaged during half a century in an all-out armaments race; or permanently throwing all its resources above a minimum of individual consumption into the checking of some natural catastrophe, such as the spread of a new deadly plague or a sudden deterioration of the climate; or perhaps deciding for reasons of equity to increase social services to a point where most of the national income would be distributed in this form—such a country would have to raise the level of taxation permanently to a level approaching a hundred per cent. While this would make any rational allocation of resources impossible, resources would nevertheless have to be allocated, even though we would have no more than vague guesses on which to base such allocation. A schedule once adopted would probably be carried on indefinitely, since there could be no rational way of improving on it. What kind of economic administration would be adopted, we cannot tell and need not discuss here. One conclusion only interests us here: that the market and the whole system of civil law that governs it would disappear. There would be no room for economic liberty, property, contractual obligations, nor for the whole edifice of law and jurisprudence, the greater part of which is concerned with property and contractual obligations.

STATUS OF PUBLIC LIBERTIES

Is then public liberty in no way a purpose in itself? Obviously not insofar as it is a method for the social management of a given economic task. We are not however inescapably bound to any particular economic task and may conceivably prefer a state of relative poverty in which we can maintain a freer economic order. Opulence and even the instruments of defence are not altogether overriding requirements of national life. Economic tasks cannot even be rationally formulated, without presupposing a society in which other purposes than those of satisfying the senses are also embodied; as no society can be based exclusively on the sensual appetites of its members. Nor can any nation survive morally, and in the end physically, by ruthlessly exploiting its armed power. National greatness depends as much on generosity as on force; the most important gains were achieved by nations when they risked their vital interests by exercising moral restraint in their relation to other nations. A nation may indeed have to court disaster in upholding its moral nature if it is to avoid surviving as a kind of people it does not want to be. Hence, economic tasks—whether aiming at the acquisition of wealth or the instruments of defence—are never rigidly given; on the contrary, the rational acceptance of an economic task must always fully weigh up its social implications. The necessity of making marginal day-to-day choices between economic efficiency and economic liberty has been pointed out already in the previous section.

OTHER EXAMPLES

Public liberty can be fully upheld as an aim in itself, insofar as it is the method for the social management of purposes
that are aims in themselves. Freedom of science, freedom of
worship, freedom of thought in general, are public institutions by which society opens to its members the opportunity
for serving aims that are purposes in themselves. By establishing these freedoms, society constitutes itself as a community of people believing in the validity and power of things of
the mind and in our obligation to these things. Logically, the
acceptance of these beliefs is anterior to freedom. There is
no justification for demanding freedom of thought unless
you believe that thought has a power of its own. Yet it is true
that in the mental development of some people in our own
days the causal sequence was often reversed. They first discovered that they could no longer bear to repeat lies and
must contradict, and only later realized that this implied a belief in the possibility of knowing the truth and the obligation
of telling it. The forceful repudiation of Communism by
many Western writers formerly sympathetic to it, which occurred in the years following the Moscow trials of 1936–38,
has made the re-establishment of absolute values the pre-
eminent concern of these writers. The first protest Tito
raised against Moscow was that the Party cannot overrule
truth. Generally speaking, it was the fall of liberty in Europe
that startled the West into a new consciousness of the beliefs
on which these liberties stand. But the beliefs remain nevertheless logically prior to these liberties.

CRITIQUE OF PUBLIC LIBERTIES

If this is the ground on which public liberties seek to justify
themselves, then they inevitably incur, on their own showing, a threefold charge which has in fact been steadily lev-
elled at them from the totalitarian standpoint. It appears

238

that the conduct of public affairs by this method; 1. surrenders the public good to the personal decisions and motives of individuals; 2. thus submits society to the rule of a privileged oligarchy; and 3. allows at the same time society to drift in a direction willed by no one.

Let me put the case for these several charges.

(1) Individuals, whether producers or consumers, who find their livelihood by operating in a market, are engaged in the competitive pursuit of personal gain. Scientists, judges, scholars, ministers of religion, etc., are guided by systems of thought to the growth, application or dissemination of which they are dedicated; their actions are determined by their professional interests. All these persons engaged in forming various systems of spontaneous order, are guided by their standard incentives which do not aim at promoting the welfare of the social body as a whole. The business man must seek profit, the judge find the law, the scientist pursue discovery, for that is what makes him a business man, a judge, or a scientist as the case may be—of the manner in which his action affects the public good as a whole he is ignorant, nor could he allow himself to be deflected by such knowledge if he possessed it, from the performance of his professional duty.[26]

26. For a more general discussion of this point I wish to quote again my article, "The Growth of Thought in Society," (*Economica* 1941): ". . . inherent in the mechanical nature of social organizations is the divergence between the standard motive of the individual and the purpose of the whole, in which he participates. A subordinate working for a corporation has to be careful and disciplined in his duties but beyond that the interests of the corporation which he serves are not his concern. His attention is properly due to the detail entrusted to him and to the exact intentions of his superior; his legitimate incentive is to gain promotion by pleasing his superior. The corporation must be so organized and directed that an employee will advance its interests best by following this line of action. The position of the individual partaking in a system of spontaneous order

(2) Great power is exercised over the public good by such individuals. Under capitalism, business men handle the major part of the nation's wealth and direct the day-to-

---

is similar. The problem before him comprises his entire responsibility. To the solution of his own problem, to the fulfilment of his own special task, he owes his entire devotion. The rules by which he has to be guided in doing so and by which he has to gain public approval for his achievements, must be such as to safeguard the advancement of the spontaneous order, whenever individual actions are taken in compliance with them.

The official character of the employee or public official, as distinct from his private person, and the limitations set upon his intentions by discipline, are usually known well enough. But the official character of the person acting independently of the public individual partaking in a dynamic system, is not commonly recognized as clearly.

Economic science has analysed the situation with respect to a system of competitive production. The standard incentives of the individual producer have been defined and his normal obligations considered, as distinct from his private motives inducing him to pursue those incentives and to accept those obligations. It is also clear that he has no responsibility for the advancement of national or planetary prosperity in general, which is the purpose of the system, taken as a whole, in which he participates. He may try to reform business life, both as a pioneer at his own works or as a voter or writer, etc. He may give all his earnings to charities or to the Communist Party; but he cannot carry on in business unless he keeps—while at his job—to the pursuit of profits for his firm.

The double distinction between private motives and standard motives, and between these and a general purpose, is evident in judicial procedure. A man coming forth to give evidence may be prompted by a variety of motives; a barrister may take up a case for the love of money or to please his vanity, or for political reasons, or from compassion; a judge may be guided in his career by ambition, love of juridical scholarship, etc. But once counsel has been briefed, the judge has taken the chair, witness has been sworn in, each of them falls into the pattern of his official motives. To these they must restrict themselves: keeping out not only their private inclinations, but also any attempt to aim directly at the higher purpose in which they are participating. Witness must stick to facts and must not plead; counsel must argue his case and not assume a judicial attitude; the judge must apply the law, even though he should desire to amend it."

day activities of the people engaged in producing it. The social interests entrusted to an independent judiciary and those affected by the free pursuit of science are no less momentous. Indeed, the mental activities cultivated by various branches of the writing profession—poets, journalists, philosophers, novelists, preachers, historians, economists—are perhaps the most decisive in shaping public affairs and sealing the fate of society. Viewed in this light the activities of persons engaged in the competitive, consultative and persuasive adjustments which constitute our systems of spontaneous order, may well appear as the regime of an oligarchy usurping public power. The personal advantages possessed by this oligarchy in virtue of its position may make their irresponsible prerogatives the more invidious. Particularly, since the inheritance of property and the enhanced opportunities offered to the children of more highly placed parents, tend to make their position of power and privilege hereditary within a restricted class of families; the class which under the influence of Marxism has become known as the bourgeoisie. It is in this sense that Western public liberties may be described as "bourgeois liberties," under which the public interest is withdrawn from the control of the State only to be submitted to the control of an irresponsible bourgeois oligarchy.

(3) Though the members of the "oligarchy" who primarily make use of the public liberties in Western society draw considerable benefit from this function, the fact remains that the systems of spontaneous order formed by their individual activities are moving as a whole in directions not specifically willed by them or anyone else. Public liberties constitute a system of self-co-ordination under which society moves towards unknown destinations.

Take economic life. It is of course true to say that "In 1938 Britain produced X million tons of steel and Y million tons of coal," but only in the sense in which it is correct to say: "This morning Britain shaved 10 million faces and blew 40 million noses." These things happened in Britain because the people concerned had reason to do them, not because any comprehensive intention had willed them to do so. They would be represented as so willed in a "planned economy," where the tons of steel and coal to be produced are among the favourite "production targets." Such targets, however, like the plans of which they form part, are little more than figments of the mind.[27]

Again, in the jurisdiction of the courts a well organized process goes on which is distinct and often contrary to the public interest as conceived by the State; while its consequences may not be desired by the courts either, nor even foreseen by them. When the lawyers and the courts of law successfully denied to the Stuarts in England the King's right to sit in his own court, they won a political victory, but not for themselves. They established the supremacy of the law over the monarch. When the seven bishops indicted for libel by James II were acquitted by a court of law, the monarchy was shaken because it had come into conflict with this principle, operating impersonally. Similarly, the acquittal under Louis XVI of Cardinal de Rohan (involved in the necklace affair) by the Parliament of Paris gave the signal to the French Revolution, which that Parliament could never have dreamt of and would have abhorred if it had. The acquittal in 1878 of Vera Zasulitch who shot General Trepow, or of Dimitrov in 1933 accused of firing the Reichstag, were all acts of an independent judiciary, conflicting with the public interest as seen by the responsible executive, and fraught with unforeseen and indeed altogether unpredictable consequences. The legal

27. See pp. 164–69 above.

theory of modern authoritarianism sets out to eliminate such contradictions, by denying validity to any legal rule insofar as it conflicts with the executive policy of the government.[28] But insofar as this policy is put into effect it abolishes in fact the rule of law and the liberty of the citizen under the law.

The State which subsidizes scientific research aims at the advancement of science; but the ensuing discoveries are unpremeditated and indeed unforeseeable. So long as science is free, humanity is travelling at its peril towards unknown destinations. The discovery of atomic fission at the end of 1938 has led within six and a half years to the construction of the atomic bomb, which has so far failed to wreck humanity only because of the extreme technical difficulty of manufacturing these bombs. If some further discovery would make atomic bombs readily available, so that any small plant could make one at the cost of £10, the threat to the community from criminals or subversive individuals, who might get hold of such weapons, would become so intense that only the strictest supervision of the entire human race by one central police authority could sustain the continued existence of humanity on the planet. Yet to guard against such dangers by planning the progress of science, so that it may yield only results that are socially desirable, is impossible. To "plan" science is to suppress it; and in this sense only could the "planning of science" protect us from the consequences of scientific progress.

28. Compare e.g., J. W. Jones, *Historic Introduction to the Theory of Law* (1940), Chapter XI. A recent news-item may serve to illustrate the point. The *Manchester Guardian* reports on 25th September, 1949, from Prague that "Mr. Harvey Moore, a British guest at the Czechoslovak Lawyers' Congress here, was promptly denounced by the Czech Deputy Minister of Justice, Dr. Dressler, as 'an old-fashioned bourgeois reactionary' when he advocated the independence of lawyers and judges."

These are heavy accusations against the management of society by spontaneous order. In the next section I shall try to say what I can in reply to them and to other criticisms of liberty, brought up by previous parts of this essay.

THE DEFENCE OF LIBERTY

The logic of public liberty is to co-ordinate independent individual actions spontaneously in the service of certain tasks. We were led to face up to the possibility that some of the tasks pursued by modern society may have in future to be abandoned. The economic task of society may be re-set in response to quite novel technical developments, in a manner which would eliminate the market and much of our judicial system. The day may come when the free pursuit of natural science may have to be curbed. There are many ways in which the most precious liberties of to-day may cease to be relevant or even admissible.

But I doubt whether by such speculations we can gain any true guidance for ourselves or give any to later generations. We cannot foresee sufficiently the manner in which, and the extent to which, the technological setting of public liberties is likely to change. I have said before in this book that our primary aim must be to form a good society, respecting truth and justice, and cultivating love between fellow-citizens. The holding of the ultimate beliefs which constitute the good society, should make to-day such a society both good and free. I trust that in seeking to establish a good society, man is fulfilling his transcendent obligation and that it is right to accept as inscrutable the ultimate ends to which this may lead.

For we *are* adrift; subject to the hazards of this universe whose future is unknown to us. The recent rise of man from the ranks of the animals, his brief effort at civilized life, his luminous creative achievements through which he has come to see himself in the perspective of space, time and history—these are events which leave undeclared their ultimate origin and future course. The conceptions by the light of which men will judge our own ideas in a thousand years—or perhaps even in fifty years—are beyond our guess. If a library of the year 3000 came into our hands to-day, we could not understand its contents. How should we consciously determine a future which is, by its very nature, beyond our comprehension? Such presumption reveals only the narrowness of an outlook uninformed by humility. The super-planner who—like Engels in the passionate declaration of the "Anti-Dühring"—announces that men "with full consciousness will fashion their own history" and "leap from the realm of necessity into the realm of freedom," reveals the megalomania of a mind rendered unimaginative by abandoning all faith in God. When such men are eventually granted power to control the ultimate destinies of their fellow men, they reduce them to mere fodder for their unbridled enterprises. And presently illusions of grandeur turn into illusions of persecution, and convert the planning of history into a reign of terror.

The logic which prevents man from controlling the drift of history also limits the possibility of eliminating the oligarchic system under which a free society achieves its aims. The tasks which can be achieved only by independent mutual adjustments demand an institutional framework which will uphold independent positions. The holders of such positions will have to pursue the standard obligations and incentives of their positions, turning a blind eye on the public interest as a whole; while the higher type of ability which the performance of such independent functions often requires will inevitably possess a scarcity value, for which members of the "oligarchy" will be able to extract a substantial price in the form of fees, salaries, profits, etc.

Seen in this perspective, such a system of privileges should be acceptable, particularly if combined with equality of opportunities. At any rate, its continued existence seems indispensable, until social solidarity achieves as yet unexplored levels of sensibility. Our desire for complete brotherhood among men must always make allowance for the requirements of the social machinery. Where members of the bourgeoisie helped into power a regime—like that of Lenin or Hitler—which destroyed or greatly reduced their own privileges, their class was invariably replaced by a servile praetorian guard, enjoying no fewer privileges while suppressing or perverting the great heritage which the bourgeoisie had cultivated throughout the period of its ascendancy.

Those who would break up a society which can be operated only by the interplay of independent, narrow and often purely selfish individual aims, should ponder on it that the elimination of the existing shortcomings of our society may bring about immeasurably greater evil. However often this kind of warning may have proved false in the past, its principle is still true. It remains in the last resort for each of us in his own conscience to balance the perils of complacency against those of recklessness. The danger that such ultimate decision may prove erroneous seems to me comparatively slight, so long as we continue humbly to search for guidance on matters over which we can never hope to achieve ultimate mastery.

Bibliography

SELECTED WRITINGS OF MICHAEL POLANYI

The Contempt of Freedom. London: C. A. Watts, 1940.

"The Growth of Thought in Society." *Economica* 8 (November 1941): 428–56.

Science, Faith and Society. London: Oxford University Press, 1946.

Personal Knowledge. Chicago: University of Chicago Press, 1958 (The Gifford Lectures, 1951–52).

Beyond Nihilism. London: Cambridge University Press, 1960.

"History and Hope: An Analysis of Our Age." *Virginia Quarterly Review* 38 (Spring 1962): 177–95.

The Tacit Dimension. Garden City, N.Y.: Doubleday, 1966.

Society, Economics & Philosophy: Selected Papers [from 1917–70]. Edited with an introduction by R. T. Allen. New Brunswick, N.J.: Transaction Publishers, 1997. This volume contains an extensive annotated bibliography of Polanyi's political and philosophical writings.

Michael Polanyi Papers. Special Collections. University of Chicago. Joseph Regenstein Library.

SELECTED SECONDARY WRITINGS

Gelwick, Richard. *The Way of Discovery: An Introduction to the Thought of Michael Polanyi.* New York: Oxford University Press, 1977.

Prosch, Harry. *Michael Polanyi: A Critical Exposition.* Albany: State University of New York Press, 1986.

Allen, Richard. *Polanyi.* London: Claridge Press, 1990.

Index

INDEX

INDEX

INDEX

INDEX

INDEX

The typeface for the text of this book is Baskerville. Its creator, John Baskerville (1706–75), was successful in many enterprises, but his type designs and his printing business were exceptions. He broke with tradition, creating designs that were more refined and delicate than those of his predecessors and in order to print them accurately made improvements in his presses and had paper specially made for his needs. His work, a true labor of love, was much criticized by his contemporaries, and his designs virtually disappeared until the early years of this century. Baskerville's designs and those derived from them are now considered among the most beautiful and useful we have.

This book is printed on paper that is acid-free and meets the requirements of the American National Standard for Permanence of Paper for Printed Library Materials, Z39.48-1992. ∞

Book design by Betty Binns

Composition by Douglas & Gayle Limited, Indianapolis, Indiana

Printed and bound by Edwards Brothers Malloy, Inc., Ann Arbor, Michigan